COMPLETE GUIDE
TO FIDUCIARY ACCOUNTING

J. G. Denhardt, Jr., CPA
John D. Grider, CPA

COMPLETE GUIDE TO
FIDUCIARY ACCOUNTING

Prentice-Hall, Inc.
Englewood Cliffs, N.J.

Prentice-Hall International, Inc., *London*
Prentice-Hall of Australia, Pty. Ltd., *Sydney*
Prentice-Hall of Canada, Ltd., *Toronto*
Prentice-Hall of India Private Ltd., *New Delhi*
Prentice-Hall of Japan, Inc., *Tokyo*
Prentice-Hall of Southeast Asia Pte. Ltd., *Singapore*
Whitehall Books, Ltd., *Wellington, New Zealand*

This publication is designed to provide accurate and authoritative information with regard to the subject matter covered. It is sold with the understanding that the publisher is not engaged in rendering legal, accounting, or other professional advice. If legal advice or other expert assistance is required, the services of a competent professional person should be sought.

— From a Declaration of Principles jointly adopted by a Committee of the American Bar Association and a Committee of Publishers and Associations.

Library of Congress Cataloging in Publication Data

Denhardt, J G
    Complete guide to fiduciary accounting.

    Includes index.
        1. Trusts and trustees—United States—Accounting.
I. Grider, John D., joint author.   II. Title.
III. Title: Fiduciary accounting.
HF5686.T8D46   657′.47   80-28061
ISBN 0-13-160572-0

Printed in the United States of America

ABOUT THE AUTHORS

J. G. Denhardt, Jr., CPA, is a member of the American Institute of CPAs and the Kentucky Society of CPAs. He is the author of *Complete Guide to Estate Accounting and Taxes* and *Complete Guide to Trust Accounting and Trust Income Taxation*, both published by Prentice-Hall, Inc., *Everyone's Guide to Estate Planning*, published by Contemporary Books, Inc., and *Fiduciary Accounting Seminar*, published by the American Institute of CPAs. He has also written a number of articles which have appeared in professional publications, including two in the *Journal of Accountancy*.

Mr. Denhardt is an individual accounting practitioner in Bowling Green, Kentucky, and he has also taught accounting and taxation at Western Kentucky University on a part-time basis since 1947.

He has served numerous times as discussion leader for professional development seminars for accountants in the estate field, and he is a former member of the Editorial Advisory Board of the *Journal of Accountancy*, of the Board of the Kentucky Society of CPAs, and of the Kentucky State Board of Accountancy.

He was graduated with a B.S. degree from Western Kentucky University in 1935 and received his B.S. in Accounting from Bowling Green College of Commerce in 1936.

* * * * *

John D. Grider, CPA, is a graduate of the Bowling Green College of Commerce and a member of the American Institute of CPAs and the Kentucky Society of CPAs.

For a number of years he was a public accounting practitioner, serving as a partner in a firm in Bowling Green, Kentucky.

Since 1976 he has been employed as Executive Vice President and Senior Trust Officer of the Citizens National Bank in Bowling Green, Kentucky.

Mr. Grider has served as discussion leader for professional development seminars for accountants in the estate and trust fields.

A Word from the Authors

Fiduciary accounting is an important area of knowledge for the accountant who has estates and trusts as clients; but even though he has no fiduciary clients at present, an accountant should prepare for the time when he might need to know the type of accounting required for executors, administrators, trustees, guardians, committees, and possibly receivers.

There are a number of important differences in fiduciary accounting and ordinary commercial accounting, and the accountant who is called upon by an executor, trustee, or other fiduciary to establish and maintain the accounting records for the fiduciary must be well aware of these differences.

Fiduciary accounting is unique because many of the rules, principles, and concepts vary from state to state and sometimes even within the counties of a state, and it is unique because many of the actions taken by the fiduciary, including some that will affect the accounting, are governed not by state or federal laws but by the wishes of the decedent or grantor as expressed in the will or trust instrument.

An accountant is often engaged by an executor or trustee who is a friend or relative of the decedent or grantor and who has no experience in his duties as a fiduciary. This person will expect his accountant to know not only the proper way of handling the accounting records but also something about the duties of the fiduciary based on whatever laws are applicable or on the creator's wishes as set forth in the governing instrument. He will expect guidance from his accountant throughout every phase of the administration. This book, therefore, presents a complete coverage of fiduciary duties as well as fiduciary accounting.

The greatly increasing number of large estates and the more extensive use of trusts makes it much more likely than in the past that the average accountant will need to know these things. And accountants themselves are likely to be called upon to be an executor or a trustee.

This book focuses on the operations of a fiduciary and the accountant's important role in maintaining the proper accounting records needed to protect the fiduciary, to have all necessary information available at all times, and to provide the proper information for the required reports to the beneficiaries and to the court. This will enable the practitioner to start providing an important service to his fiduciary clients, a service he is likely to be called upon to do much more than in the past.

Fortunately, there are many more similarities between commercial accounting and fiduciary accounting than differences, as important as those differences are. As a result, fiduciary accounting is not difficult. In many ways it is even more simple than other accounting.

The similarities and the differences are explained thoroughly in the first chapter of this book. This is followed by a detailed description of the actual bookkeeping system that might be established for a fiduciary, including examples. And, since one of the principal objectives of fiduciary accounting is to provide information for any required reports, a discussion of the form and content of reports is given, also with examples.

Accounting and reporting for an estate is discussed in detail and is illustrated by a case study in estate accounting. There is also a discussion of accounting for a trust, in which the peculiarities of trust accounting are emphasized, and a case study in trust accounting is given.

But although the book focuses principally on the accounting for an individual executor or trustee, and on his duties, there is also included information on other fiduciaries, such as guardians, committees, agents, and receivers.

And although the individual fiduciary is covered in more detail, the fact that a very great number of fiduciary duties are performed by trust companies rather than by individuals is recognized, so there is included a section on the accounting methods generally used by these trust companies. It is pointed out that although the actual forms, systems, and methods used by trust companies are very different from those used by an individual, the same principles of fiduciary accounting apply and the system must be designed to provide the same information.

This book includes all the essential information about fiduciaries and fiduciary accounting needed to lead an accountant into an interesting, new, lucrative area of practice and to make him much more expert and at ease when working in this field.

We wish to express our appreciation to the American Institute of CPAs for granting us permission to adapt some of the materials from their seminar on *Fiduciary Accounting* and to Prentice-Hall, Inc., for permission to make use of some of their published materials, particularly *Complete Guide to Estate Accounting and Taxes* and *Complete Guide to Trust Accounting and Trust Income Taxation.*

J. G. Denhardt, Jr.
John D. Grider

Table of Contents

COMPLETE GUIDE
TO FIDUCIARY ACCOUNTING

CHAPTER One

Fiduciary Accounting in General

1

Fiduciary accounting is a specialized area of accounting, as there are several very important differences between fiduciary accounting and ordinary commercial accounting. Still, there are many more similarities than differences between the two, and as a result, fiduciary accounting is not really difficult. In many ways it is even easier than other accounting.

The principal cause of difficulty is its relative unfamiliarity to most accountants. But the accountant who learns to recognize and understand the few differences required by good fiduciary accounting, and who is familiar with the duties and responsibilities of a fiduciary, will be able to design and maintain just as good a bookkeeping system for a fiduciary as he could for any other entity.

A fiduciary accounting system will have the same kinds of books and the same double-entry bookkeeping system as any other business might have. There is no standard accounting system for a fiduciary. And, as with other businesses, fiduciaries vary so much in size and complexity that the books for each one should be designed and maintained with that particular one in mind. As a result, there might be as much difference between the systems for different fiduciaries as there would be between those for a small local store and a large industrial corporation.

However, there are a number of account titles and a number of new concepts not found in commercial accounting. The fiduciary accountant must become completely familiar with these, and each will be explained in detail in this book. And of course he must know exactly what a fiduciary is and have a good understanding of a fiduciary's duties and responsibilities.

What Is a Fiduciary?

A fiduciary is a person (or a trust company) who has agreed to accept the legal ownership and the control and management of an asset, or a group of assets, belonging to someone else.

In accepting this responsibility he also agrees to manage the assets in exact accordance with the wishes of the person who established the fiduciary relationship.

In the case of an estate, the fiduciary is known as an executor (or an administrator). He is responsible for administering the decedent's estate assets in whatever way the decedent might have directed in his will. If the will does not contain complete enough instructions in every area, state law takes over and gives the needed instructions. The executor must, in almost every case, make periodic reports of the progress of his administration to the probate court, and he also has a responsibility to the estate's beneficiaries to administer and finally distribute the assets as directed in the will and by state law. If the decedent died without a will, the fiduciary, known as an administrator in this case, must follow the directions of state and local law in carrying out the administration and must finally distribute the estate assets in the way provided by his state's laws regarding descent and distribution.

In the case of a trust, the fiduciary is known as a trustee, and his directions are contained in the written instrument creating the trust, or, in the case of a testamentary trust, in the provisions of the decedent's will establishing the trust. Each of these will be supplemented by state and local law where necessary.

A trustee's operations are not always subject to review by a court, as a trust instrument does not necessarily even have to be recorded in the public records. His responsibility is primarily to the beneficiaries of the trust who, of course, have the right to take any questionable acts of the trustee to court.

A fiduciary is given *legal title* to the estate or trust assets, but he does not acquire *equitable title* to them. He acquires only the legal title necessary for the administration of the assets; the assets do not become his, but are his for only a temporary period and for a specific purpose. Equitable ownership at all times belongs to others.

Although this book focuses primarily on the fiduciary accounting for an executor or trustee, it should be mentioned that there are several other kinds of fiduciaries, such as agents, committees, guardians, and receiverships; these are described in detail in a later chapter.

The Fiduciary's Powers

It is obvious from the above discussion of his role that the fiduciary is a key figure, as well as a necessary one, in any trust or estate.

A good fiduciary, one able to do whatever job is required by the particular administration, is an absolute necessity for a good, effective administration. The duties vary greatly in different cases; sometimes very little is required of the fiduciary, but in other cases the administration could be a full time job requiring much knowledge and ability. And although the fiduciary's operations are sometimes under the supervision of the court, his day-to-day decisions can have very important consequences, and they could possibly result in unnecessary expense and difficulties even though he might have done nothing really illegal.

A fiduciary has only those powers given to him by a testator or grantor and those vested in him by statutes, rules of equity, or court orders. The grantor's intent in respect to his fiduciary's powers and authority may be expressly stated in the instrument or may be implied in the general language of the instrument setting forth the purposes of the estate or trust. But, in general, the fiduciary will be considered to have all powers "necessary and appropriate" to accomplish those purposes, even though not specifically given to him, unless any are forbidden by the terms of the trust.

One of the most important powers a fiduciary could have would be the power to sell the property. If the instrument gives or withholds this power, that, of course, governs. If the instrument is silent regarding borrowing against the trust property, there is generally no such power implied; however, a court might authorize borrowing in emergencies if it seems desirable in order to preserve the property and is consistent with the grantor's probable wishes.

A fiduciary does have the implied power to incur reasonable expenses in the administration of the property, including the power to make improvements on the property when necessary to preserve the assets.

The Fiduciary's Duties

Subject to the general rules and any specific instructions, a fiduciary's powers are very broad. Still, they are accompanied by many duties.

He has the duty, of course, to administer his office in accordance with the terms of the instrument governing him. He must do this with the degree of care and skill which a "reasonably prudent businessman" would use in dealing with his own property, and, if he has any special skills, he is expected to use them as well. His primary duty is to preserve the property under his control rather than to make it produce income, but since the purpose of most fiduciary relationships, especially with trusts, is the production of income, that follows closely as another prime objective.

He has a duty to keep his own funds and assets entirely separate from those of the trust; he cannot make a personal loan to the trust and he cannot borrow from the trust, even if he agrees to pay interest on the loan. He may not accept any bonus or commission from any third person for any of his actions in connection with his trust.

A fiduciary has a duty to examine the terms of the creating instrument to ascertain the property comprising its subject matter, the identity of the beneficiaries, and his own duties as fiduciary. He next has a duty to take tangible real or personal property into his possession and to take the steps necessary to secure the ownership of any documents representing intangible assets, such as savings account passbooks. In doing so he may make whatever use of agents and others as is reasonable in view of the type of property and the other circumstances of the case. He must use reasonable diligence to discover the location of the property that should come to him and to take control of it without unnecessary delay. If the trust was created by the grantor during his lifetime, the grantor will ordinarily deliver the property to the trustee, but if he does not the trustee must hold the grantor to this obligation. If the trust is set up by will, the property will come to the trustee through the executor, and the trustee must require the executor to turn over the assets to him as soon as the will and probate law permit.

A fiduciary must use reasonable care and prudence in caring for the assets. He must see that deeds are recorded, carry adequate insurance on insurable property, rent a safe deposit box for the care of securities and other important documents, and take any other action necessary to preserve the property against theft or other loss; and he should do anything else that a prudent man would do in caring for assets, such as inspecting them from time to time, supervising all investments, paying off encumbrances and taxes that might jeopardize title, keeping properties in good repair, and others.

He has a duty to make the property produce income, so he must develop a program to secure income from the assets or to sell any nonproductive assets (if he has this power) and reinvest the proceeds in other assets that do produce.

The Fiduciary's Responsibilities

The fiduciary's office must be administered solely for the benefit of the beneficiaries, and the fiduciary is not permitted to take any position that could conceivably be adverse to theirs. He must never obtain any personal advantage at the expense of the beneficiaries. These self-interest rules are so strict that a corporate fiduciary cannot invest trust funds in its own stock and, in most cases, it cannot even retain such shares if placed in trust by the grantor himself, unless the trust instrument specifically provides for the purchase or retention of the shares. The fiduciary is under a duty of absolute loyalty to the beneficiaries, and the law is extremely zealous in enforcing this relationship.

Further responsibilities of a fiduciary are to pay expenses promptly and not allow obligations to become delinquent; to make payments and distributions to the correct beneficiary, rather than merely to use good faith, ordinary care, or the advice of counsel; to maintain a careful segregation of principal and income to protect the interests of the principal and income beneficiaries; to maintain adequate accounting records (considered so important that it has even been held that a provision in a trust instrument saying that the trustee need not keep accounts *may* manifest an intention not to create a trust); to pay a decedent's debts; to defend any suits against the estate or trust, if there is any defense available, and to prosecute suits in favor of the estate or trust; to prepare and file any required reports to the court and the beneficiaries; and to pay any income, estate, or inheritance taxes due.

It is apparent from the preceding paragraphs that a fiduciary has a great amount of responsibility and that there are many acts that could cause him to be personally liable to the beneficiaries or even to third persons. Still, if a fiduciary fulfills his office with complete good faith and prudence he stands very little chance of personal liability; if he does not, his liability can be very great indeed.

For a more in-depth study of the duties and responsibilities of a fiduciary, the Uniform Fiduciary Act and the Uniform Trustees' Powers Act, both given in the Appendix, should be read.

The Fiduciary Accountant's Duties

An individual fiduciary is often a friend or relative of the decedent or trust grantor who has had no experience in this difficult field. He is frequently more or less unfamiliar with his duties as such and with fiduciary procedures in general, so he will probably call on his accountant, as well as his lawyer, almost daily for assistance in administrative problems and procedures, in addition to the accounting and tax questions.

The accountant for the fiduciary must, therefore, become familiar with the administrative procedures applicable to his particular case to be of most service to his client.

He must, first, make a thorough study of the will or trust instrument that governs his client, and he should ask the client's attorney for interpretations of any provisions not clear to him.

Next, if his fiduciary is an executor or administrator, he must be familiar with local probate practices and procedures, such as probating the will, publishing a notice to creditors, taking possession of the assets, opening the lockbox, filing the estate inventory, the duties of the appraisers, payment of claims, distributions to the beneficiaries, and others.

If the fiduciary is a trustee, the accountant should be able to advise him, in a general way at least, as to his powers under the governing instrument and state law. He should be able to give his fiduciary advice about obtaining the trust property, caring for the assets, management of the assets, the use of discretion, the delegation of authority, the payment of expenses and distributions, and others.

In any case, the accountant's general business background and experience should be of value in advising the fiduciary in such matters as whether or not he should open an office, whether to keep a going business in operation if a part of the assets, timing the payment of expenses and distributions, and the like.

The accountant must be well versed in estate taxation and the income taxation of estates and trusts, and he should be able to point out any tax-saving opportunities during the course of the administration.

Finally, of course, he must know good fiduciary accounting methods and procedures and be able to design and maintain a set of accounting records that will fit his particular fiduciary's case, and he must be able to prepare any necessary reports of the administration for the court or the beneficiaries.

Purposes of the Accounting System

The purposes of a fiduciary accounting system are, as with the system for any other entity, to provide control over the assets, to furnish a detailed historical record of the transactions, and to enable the fiduciary to obtain quickly and accurately whatever financial information he might need in his administration of the assets.

The system must also furnish protection for the fiduciary. A fiduciary holds a position of trust and responsibility, and all of his operations are likely to be observed with a critical eye by the beneficiaries to whom he is responsible and, in many cases, by a court of law. A good system can help furnish this protection by showing, at any time, the exact disposition of any assets turned over to the fiduciary, the income earned and its source, the expenditures, the cash and other assets on hand, and the amounts available for distribution to the various beneficiaries.

The system must be designed in a way that will facilitate the preparation of reports, reports to the beneficiaries and to the court, which the fiduciary must furnish from time to time. To do this, it must show complete information about the assets turned over to the fiduciary, increases and decreases in these assets, income and expenses, and distributions of income or of assets.

And, since the preparation of correct tax returns is one of the principal duties of a fiduciary, the accounting system must be designed in such a way that the information needed for the fiduciary income tax return and, in the case of an estate, for the estate and inheritance tax returns, will be readily available. It might be mentioned here that although "pure" fiduciary accounting does not take tax requirements into consideration, a good fiduciary accounting system will provide the figures to which the necessary adjustments can be made to arrive at the correct figures for tax purposes.

> Fiduciary accounting is unique. Unlike commercial accounting, which is governed by and based upon generally accepted accounting principles, fiduciary accounting concepts are determined by state law. As a result, there are conflicts between fiduciary accounting and commercial accounting. And there are further differences between fiduciary accounting and tax accounting. But by following good, standard fiduciary accounting principles, the accountant will produce results that can be easily reconciled, if necessary, with commercial accounting or with tax accounting.

The Uniform Trustees Accounting Act, included in the Appendix, should be studied for a greater understanding of the purposes and objectives of fiduciary accounting.

Principal and Income

With the preceding as background, it might be good now to consider the several important features peculiar to fiduciary accounting.

The main point of difference between fiduciary accounting and ordinary commercial accounting is caused by the absolute necessity for keeping the books in such a way as to distinguish clearly between the principal (or corpus) of the estate or trust and its income, at all times.

The distinction between principal and income is necessary because in most cases the decedent's will, or the trust instrument, designates one person to receive the income (a life tenant, perhaps) and another to receive the principal (a remainderman); and even though it may not be necessary under the creating document to make such distinctions, the requirements of estate, inheritance, and income tax laws usually make it desirable, if not mandatory, to do so. So the accounting system must be kept in such a way that at any time the amount accruing to each of the two classes of beneficiaries may be readily determined.

Example of Principal and Income

A simple example might help to clarify the differences between transactions affecting principal and those affecting income. Suppose the fiduciary's only assets are non-income producing property—a vacant house, its furnishings, a vacant lot, and cash in the bank. If the vacant lot is sold for the amount at which it was placed on the books, one asset (the lot) is simply exchanged for another (cash or a receivable), and neither principal nor income is affected. If the lot is sold for more than its book figure, the terms of the governing instrument or state law must be consulted to see whether such a gain is to be considered as income or as an increase in the principal of the fiduciary. If cash is spent in paying a decedent's debts, estate administration expenses, and so on, principal is decreased but income is not affected—such expenditures are properly considered as deductions from principal rather than from income (in the case of an estate); and, obviously, in this case there is no income from which they may be deducted.

But suppose that the vacant house is rented to a tenant; the rent received is income. Suppose the proceeds from the sale of the vacant lot are invested in bonds; the interest on the bonds is income though the bonds themselves remain a part of the principal.

Suppose, further, that the net income accumulates in an amount that warrants its investment, and it is invested in bonds. These bonds do not become principal; they are still part of the assets belonging to the income beneficiaries, and the income they produce belongs to income also.

The legal theory seems to be that the principal is not a certain amount of monetary value, but is a certain group of assets which must be capable of isolation from the assets that compose the undistributed net income. These assets of the principal may change in form, or even in amount, but they always constitute the principal of the entity.

Uniform Principal and Income Act

It might be good at this point to study the Uniform Principal and Income Act, which is included in the Appendix.

The basic philosophy of this Act is that the testator or grantor can allocate receipts and expenditures in any way that he sees fit, and the function of the Act is to supply the rules of allocations between principal and income when the will or trust instrument fails to give them. Such allocations will be made after due consideration has been given to the respective interests of the income and the principal beneficiaries, and the proper procedure for recording estate and trust transactions is as follows:

1. Be certain that the provisions of the will or trust agreement are complied with.
2. The provisions of state law must be followed unless there are contrary terms in the will or trust instrument.
3. If neither the will or trust instrument, nor the state law, provides applicable provisions, fiduciary accounting treatment should adopt a reasonable and equitable approach, taking into account the interests of those entitled to income as well as those entitled to the principal, in such a manner as men of ordinary prudence, discretion, and judgment would use in the management of their own affairs.

The fiduciary must use his own judgment in protecting the rights of the two different classes of beneficiaries, but his accountant can be of great assistance in helping him to reach a reasonable and equitable determination in making the proper allocation.

Separation of Principal and Income

Actual separation of cash and other assets between those belonging to principal and those belonging to income is difficult, but ordinarily it will be sufficient to keep one account for cash and one for each type of investment, as with any other bookkeeping system, and to find a way of indicating the claims of the principal beneficiaries and the income beneficiaries in the total net assets.

This can be accomplished by a carefully planned chart of ledger accounts, one that includes *two* proprietorship accounts, one being called "Principal" and the other "Income." The fiduciary's operating income and expense will be closed into the "Income" account periodically, and this account, then, will indicate the amount of the income beneficiaries' claim to the net assets of the fiduciary. The amount in the "Principal" account will, likewise, indicate the amount of the net assets belonging to the principal beneficiaries. It is relatively unimportant just which specific assets comprise either of these two amounts, but the more liquid assets will generally be designated as assets belonging to Income—frequently only cash and any securities purchased with net income—and the remainder of the assets will be considered as belonging to Principal.

This concept of "dual proprietorship" is the principal feature distinguishing fiduciary accounting from that of all other types of business entities.

In a sole proprietorship, only one person has complete ownership of the net assets and of the income, so only one net worth account is needed. In a corporation, even though there might be thousands of stockholders, the same thing is basically true—one *group* has complete ownership, and the objectives and concerns of all those within that group are (theoretically, at least) identical; only one equity account is needed. And even in a partnership the two or more partners have the same, though possibly disproportionate, interests in the assets and in the income, and the same objectives; even though there are two or more proprietorship accounts on the books, each will be affected by each transaction in the same way.

But in a fiduciary, there is *dual ownership*. One of the owners is the income beneficiary (or a group of them) and the other is the remainderman (or a group). The interests of the two are *not* identical—most often they are conflicting. Anything that benefits one will be disadvantageous to the other. So there must be *two* proprietorship accounts, and each transaction must be carefully analyzed and recorded in a way that will insure that it will eventually affect the proper one of these accounts, based on the directions in the governing instrument and state law.

A device that is an aid in the proper segregation of principal and income is the use of two separate ledger accounts for cash—"Principal Cash" and "Income Cash"—even though there may be only one actual bank account and one checkbook. Each journal will have a pair of columns for each of these accounts; this forces the accountant to make a decision regarding the proper segregation of principal and income each time any receipt or disbursement is entered in the journals. It also results in the ledger accounts showing how much of the asset, cash, belongs to principal and how much belongs to income.

A complete illustrative chart of the accounts that might be used in a fiduciary's ledger is given in the following chapter, but here is a skeleton outline of the several sections that must be used:

Assets:
Principal Cash
Income Cash
Various Other Assets

Liabilities:
Various Liabilities, if Any

Net Worth (Principal):
Estate (or Trust) Principal
Distributions of Principal

Net Worth (Income):
Estate (or Trust) Income
Distributions of Income

Income:
Various Income Accounts

Expenses:
Various Expense Accounts

It can be seen at a glance that this arrangement of accounts is very much like that which would be found in the ledger of any commercial business. The only real difference is the use of two equity sections rather than the usual one.

To summarize, the amount of the fiduciary's net income (as determined for that particular fiduciary) must be carefully built up in the accounts, transactions affecting the principal rather than income must be recognized and excluded from income, and some way must be found of identifying the assets into which this net income has found its way.

Items Applicable to Principal

Accountants generally think of all disbursements for expenses as being deductions from income. In fiduciaries, however, there is a certain group of expenditures which do not decrease income but which represent reductions in the principal.

These non-income deductions, for an estate, include a decedent's debts and funeral expenses, administrative fees and expenses, estate and inheritance taxes, and, of course, the payment of legacies and other distributions of principal.

As for a trust, it is possible (and not too unusual) for a trust instrument to specify whether certain administrative expenses shall be charged to principal or to income or in part to each, and for fiduciary accounting purposes such specifications will govern. In the absence of such directions, state law must be consulted to determine the proper handling of these expenditures.

But a reminder—even though certain expenses are chargeable to principal under the terms of the will, the trust instrument, or state law for the correct determination of a fiduciary's accounting income, this does not necessarily mean that they are not to be considered as expenses against income *for tax purposes.* Fees and administrative expenses, for example, are tax deductions (either estate or income tax) even though they might be considered deductions from principal for fiduciary accounting purposes, and such items are among the possibly many adjustments required later to bring fiduciary accounting income to the correct taxable income.

Items Applicable to Income

Earnings from all of the fiduciary's assets are applicable to income, regardless of whether the assets belong to principal or to income. Such earnings are those ordinarily thought of as being income—interest, dividends, rents, business profits, and others.

The expenses applicable to income are all those generally classed as ordinary operating expenses—office expense, repairs and maintenance, utilities, wages, property taxes, and so on.

The various accounts representing income and deductions from income would, if summarized into statement form, look very much like an ordinary profit and loss statement.

But again, any specific directions in the governing instrument or state law will control the deductibility of an expenditure from income or from principal, *for fiduciary accounting purposes.*

Fiduciary Accounting Income

The next requirement the accountant must keep in mind is that the books of the fiduciary must produce, at the end of each accounting period, a figure known as *Fiduciary Accounting Income.* This may seem overly obvious, but it is not. Fiduciary accounting income does not mean accounting income in the ordinary sense of the term but is the net income determined in exact accordance with whatever specific directions might be contained in the governing instrument (or state law) *for the fiduciary the system is being designed for.*

The writer of a will or the creator of a trust may spell out any terms and conditions he desires for the operation of that estate or trust. The operation of the fiduciary and its accounting system must be in complete conformity with any such provisions in the instrument, and the books must, therefore, produce the results contemplated by the writer.

Most often, the writer's prime concern (particularly for a trust) will be the amount of income he wants the fiduciary to produce for the benefit of some beneficiary, but his idea of what constitutes "income" may be far different from what is income in the general accounting sense or what is income for tax purposes.

Still, his directions must govern, and the fiduciary's books must show as net income whatever the writer has directed. This is the figure that is known as *Fiduciary Accounting Income* and is the correct income for *that particular fiduciary entity*. The fiduciary accounting income for any other fiduciary could be very different; ordinary accounting income could be different; and almost invariably taxable income will also be very different.

But it cannot be overemphasized that the accounts for any fiduciary must be designed to show the (sometimes very peculiar) income which the testator or grantor had in mind. This is the income he intended for the beneficiary to receive and, again, his wishes must be followed. If the books are kept in accordance with these principles, the fiduciary's responsibility and accountability to the income beneficiary, as well as to the remainderman, will be clear at all times. Again, the fiduciary is controlled by the terms of the governing instrument, and a good accounting system will be an invaluable aid to him in properly administering the estate or trust.

Obviously, fiduciary accounting income will almost never be the same as the taxable income which the accountant will be concerned with later. But tax considerations must be ignored completely at this point, which does present a difficulty for accountants, who are generally so tax-conscious. Still, although adjustments will have to be made later to arrive at taxable income, the starting point in determining *taxable income* is always *fiduciary accounting income*.

Cash or Accrual Basis Accounting

The principal reason why fiduciary accounting is often simpler and easier than commercial accounting is that fiduciary accounting systems almost invariably use the cash basis method rather than the accrual method of accounting.

The accrual method is permissible, but it is usually not needed and is rarely encountered. In cash basis fiduciary accounting, receivables are not recorded until they are received in cash; liabilities, also, are not recorded until they are paid. Nor are year-end accruals computed and entered on the books.

In an estate, however, amounts receivable by the decedent at the date of his death *are* recorded—but only as a part of the opening entry which includes all of his assets. Still, liabilities existing at the date of his death are *not* recorded in the opening entry; they are recorded only when paid, and a memorandum record is simply kept until that time.

Obviously, an accounting system using the cash method requires fewer records, fewer accounts, and fewer entries than one using the accrual method.

Accounting for Liabilities

Since fiduciary accounting is usually on a strict cash basis, there is seldom any need for liability accounts on the books, except possibly for those of a very current nature, such as payroll tax deductions.

For an estate, not even liabilities existing at the time of the decedent's death are recorded on the books—they are handled on a cash basis and are recorded only when paid, by a charge against the principal of the estate. This raises the question of how to account for any mortgages, installment notes, or other long-term liabilities existing at the decedent's death. These can be accounted for by memorandum records, with memo entries being made to this record for each periodic payment (excluding interest, which is a proper charge against current income). Or, contrary to the general rule, the liability can be recorded on the books with a corresponding debit to "Debts of Decedent" and handled in the ordinary way from then on.

For a trust, it is possible that mortgaged property has been turned over to the trustee. If so, the mortgage should be shown on the trust books and handled in the future according to general accounting rules.

An estate executor or a trustee may be, in a few cases, authorized to mortgage property or to otherwise borrow money in the name of the fiduciary. In the event of any such liabilities arising after the decedent's death or the creation of the trust, these liabilities will be recorded on the books and their treatment will follow ordinary accounting rules.

The Accounting Period

The accounting period for a fiduciary is a twelve-month period, as with any other entity. The executor or trustee may elect a calendar year or a fiscal year ending on the last day of any month. Two factors might enter into the decision regarding the best fiscal year to select—the time of the year at which it will be most convenient to close the books and prepare income tax returns (natural business year), and the possible desirability of having a "short" accounting period from the date of beginning to the end of the first fiscal year in order to have some of the income taxed in a lower bracket than if a full year's income were reported at one time.

The journals are posted to the ledger each month, of course, and the ledger is closed at the end of each accounting period, at which time all income and expense accounts are closed into the "Income" account. No other accounts are closed into the two net worth accounts, however, until the final closing of the books at the termination of the administration.

In short, the rules governing a fiduciary's accounting period are exactly the same as for a corporation.

Summary

A summary of the objectives and the principal features of fiduciary accounting is as follows:

1. The primary objective of fiduciary accounting is to provide a system that will distinguish clearly between the principal of the estate or trust and its income and will indicate the equity of the income and the principal beneficiaries in the net assets of the entity.

2. The distinction between principal and income is necessary because, in almost every case, there are two different classes of beneficiaries—the income beneficiaries, usually known as life tenants, and the principal beneficiaries, known as remaindermen. The different classes of beneficiaries might have conflicting interests, so it is extremely important that the accounting system show, at all times, the exact equity of each class in the fiduciary assets, in accordance with the terms of the governing instrument or state law.

3. The separation of principal and income can be accomplished by having an accounting system that includes *two* net worth accounts, one for each. By making entries to the books in accordance with good fiduciary accounting principles and in complete accordance with any instructions in the governing instrument or state law, each of the net worth accounts will, at all times, reflect the respective interests and equity of the two different classes of beneficiaries.

4. The assets comprising principal and those comprising income need not be kept physically separate or even completely separate in the accounts. It is sufficient to keep accounts for each asset and to have equity accounts which will indicate the amount of the claim each class of beneficiary has in the total assets of the fiduciary.

5. The "fiduciary accounting income" for any particular estate or trust is the net income as determined for *that particular entity* in strict accordance with any instructions contained in the decedent's will or the trust instrument or, in the absence of instructions, in accordance with state law.

6. The writer of a will or trust instrument has *complete* control over the determination of fiduciary accounting income. He may include any terms he likes and he may say that any certain item shall be considered as affecting income rather than principal, or vice versa. If he fails to take advantage of his privilege of doing this, the provisions of state law will govern.

7. Income tax provisions should be completely ignored in determining fiduciary accounting income. Adjustments to fiduciary accounting income will be made later, if necessary, to bring that figure to the correct taxable income.

8. There are seldom any liabilities included in a fiduciary's accounting books,

except for those of a current nature, as fiduciary accounting is almost invariably on a strict cash basis.

9. There can be no standard accounting system for a fiduciary because there is such a great difference in the size and complexity of different trusts and estates that there will be very little uniformity in the account titles needed, the number and kinds of journals, and so on, for different fiduciaries. But regardless of the system decided upon, the books must be designed with fiduciary accounting principles in mind and in a way that the desired and required results will be obtained from these books.

The Bookkeeping System

2

As mentioned earlier, there is no standard accounting system for a fiduciary, and there are no standard or required bookkeeping forms that any fiduciary must use.

Each set of fiduciary books should be designed with that particular fiduciary in mind and designed to accommodate the transactions expected to be needed for it. The style and complexity of a fiduciary's accounting system will depend on the volume and variety of transactions anticipated during the administration.

Many fiduciaries are so small that it would, frankly, be a waste of time to establish any set of books at all; for example, the only asset might be a single block of stock, the only income a dividend check several times a year, and the only disbursements a few checks for fees, lock box rent, a distribution to a beneficiary, or others. But other fiduciaries might contain many and varied assets and have a multitude of daily transactions, and a formal, efficient accounting system would be an absolute necessity for the protection of the executor or trustee, for making the necessary reports, for proof of the proper handling of transactions, and so on.

Still, regardless of the size of the operation or the complexity of the accounting system, the principles of fiduciary accounting must be followed, and even the fiduciary who actually needs no formal bookkeeping system at all must understand these principles and keep them in mind and follow them in the administration of his estate or trust.

This chapter on the bookkeeping system for a fiduciary is directed to the accountant establishing a system for an individual executor or trustee rather than for a corporate fiduciary. Most corporate fiduciaries (trust companies) have their own type of accounting systems, and those systems differ very greatly from the individual's system as described in this chapter. Still, their systems must follow the same basic principles and attain the same objectives as those of individual fiduciaries.

A complete study of fiduciary accounting as practiced by corporate fiduciaries is given in a later chapter, but a thorough knowledge of an individual fiduciary's accounting procedures and objectives will be most helpful before studying those of a corporate fiduciary.

Many of the procedures suggested here are based on the Uniform Trustees Accounting Act, given in the Appendix, so it might be good to read that act before proceeding further.

Books to Be Used

Although a wide variety of journals and ledgers might be used, the basic requirement, of course, is a general ledger—as with any commercial bookkeeping system. The accounts to be set up in this ledger should be very carefully planned with a view to the probable future transactions to be embraced by these accounts; as with any accounting system, common sense and the accountant's good judgment will dictate the details of the chart of accounts finally decided on. Of course, accounts might be needed in the future which cannot be anticipated at present, so a number of blank account numbers should be reserved for any of these.

The next requirement is a general journal. This journal will be needed for recording the opening entry, for recording any property of an estate discovered after the original property was entered in the books, for recording additional property turned over to a trust, for recording distributions in property rather than in cash, for making adjusting or correcting entries, for recording the closing entry, and for making any other entries that do not readily lend themselves to columnar cash journals.

A combination cash receipts-disbursements journal might be the only other book needed—a journal with columns for both cash receipts and for cash disbursements. Examples of the possible headings for the columns in such a journal are given in the case studies later in this book. Or, depending on the volume of transactions expected, two separate journals might be better—one for recording cash receipts and the other for cash disbursements. The design of the journals should cause no problem for the accountant, and the journals for a fiduciary are usually much simpler than those for other entities due to the fact that such books are almost invariably kept on a strict cash basis.

However, as suggested earlier, since the general ledger will include two cash accounts, "Principal Cash" and "Income Cash," each journal should be designed with a pair of columns for each of these rather than the usual one pair.

In some cases subsidiary ledgers might be needed. If the fiduciary has a number of assets within one category—such as stocks, bonds, or mortgages—it would certainly be desirable for the details of each specific asset to be shown separately on a subsidiary ledger page, with only a control account in the general ledger. Extensive investments in real estate, oil leases, numerous bank or brokerage accounts, and others should also be detailed in subsidiary ledgers. And although it might not be absolutely necessary, it is desirable for each subsidiary ledger sheet to be subdivided into two parts, one part for recording transactions affecting the principal of the estate or trust and the other for those affecting income.

The General Ledger

The fiduciary's general ledger should be designed to include all accounts needed at present and any others that are expected to be needed later. Particular attention should be paid to including those account titles that are peculiar to fiduciary accounting and are not found in other accounting ledgers.

It is always best to write a chart of accounts for the ledger, so that all of the accounts may be seen at a glance. As an example of such a chart, Figure 2-1 shows an Illustrative Chart of Accounts for an estate. It is highly unlikely, of course, that any one estate would need all of the accounts shown, but most of the ones possible for various fiduciaries have been included for illustrative purposes.

Although this chart is for an estate, a chart of accounts for a trust would be practically the same, with a few minor changes in account titles; these changes are pointed out in chapter 6 on accounting for a trust.

Explanation of Account Titles

A glance at the Illustrative Chart will show that a fiduciary's chart of accounts is very similar to one that any other business entity might use. It has the same five sections, for assets, liabilities, net worth, income and expenses. The only real difference is that there are *two* net worth sections, one for "Principal" and one for "Income," and that there are also two cash accounts, "Principal Cash" and "Income Cash."

This difference is necessitated, as mentioned earlier, by the extremely important requirement of fiduciary accounting principles that the income of an estate or trust must be kept entirely separate from its principal. Good fiduciary accounting accomplishes this, and, in effect, the executor or trustee is really *keeping two separate sets of books*, though they are combined into one set for convenience and practicality. As a reminder, the all-important concept of dual ownership, explained in the preceding chapter, is the basis for this fiduciary accounting requirement.

The 100 series of accounts, Assets, will cause no difficulty. As with any other asset section, accounts are set up for whatever property the fiduciary is originally charged with plus any accounts expected to be needed (such as Allowance for Depreciation). The accounts may, of course, be listed in great detail or they may be condensed. The only peculiarity in the asset section is the division of the usual cash account into two accounts, Principal Cash and Income Cash, as suggested earlier.

The Liabilities section, 200 series, might never be used, as a fiduciary seldom starts out with any liabilities. In handling the business of the entity, however, some liabilities may be incurred, but these are usually of a current character and any entries to this section will be made in accordance with ordinary accounting principles.

FIGURE 2-1

Illustrative Chart of Accounts
for an Estate

Assets:

100 - Petty Cash
101 - Principal Cash
102 - Income Cash
103 - Notes Receivable
104 - Bonds
105 - Interest Receivable
106 - Stocks
107 - Real Estate
108 - Allowance for Depreciation
109 - Rent Receivable
110 - Partnership Interest
111 - Miscellaneous Assets
112 -
113 -
114 -

Liabilities:

200 - Notes Payable
201 - Mortgage Payable
202 - Payroll Taxes Deducted
203 -
204 -

Net Worth (Principal):

300 - Estate Principal
301 - Assets Not Inventoried

401 - Debts of Decedent
402 - Funeral Expenses
403 - Administration Expenses
404 - Estate and Inheritance Taxes
405 - Gains on Realization
406 - Losses on Realization
407 - Legacies Paid
408 - Distributions of Principal

Net Worth (Income):

500 - Estate Income
600 - Distributions of Income

Income:

700 - Interest Income
701 - Dividends Received
702 - Rental Income
703 - Partnership Income
704 - Other Income
705 -
706 -
707 -
708 -

Expenses:

800 - Salaries
801 - Office Rent
802 - Office Expenses
803 - Telephone
804 - Repairs
805 - Insurance
806 - Utilities
807 - Real Estate Taxes
808 - Payroll Taxes
809 - Interest Expense
810 - Travel Expense
811 - Commissions on Collections
812 - Depreciation Expense
813 - Miscellaneous Expense
814 - Income Taxes Paid
815 -
816 -
817 -
818 -
819 -
820 -

Account number 300, Estate Principal, is the equity account, the equivalent of an investment account or a capital stock account. The concept of proprietorship, however, is almost entirely absent in fiduciaries, and its place is taken by responsibility or accountability, the amount being determined by the adjusted balance in the Estate Principal account. It is this account which is credited with the total original amount of the estate property, for which the fiduciary is accountable. Changes in the amount for which he is responsible are recorded through entires to the various accounts in the 400 series. These accounts include all expenses that are chargeable to Principal, corrections and adjustments to the original balance, and distributions of principal. They will all finally be closed into the Estate Principal account, but this is not usually done periodically. These accounts are left open until the final closing of the books, at which time (after final distribution of the assets) they are closed into Estate Principal and should entirely eliminate the balance in the Estate Principal account. At any time prior to final closing, the amount for which the fiduciary is responsible to the principal beneficiaries can be determined by combining the balances in all of the 300 and 400 series accounts. The net credit balance must be supported by net assets belonging to Principal.

The other equity, or accountability, account is Estate Income. A credit balance in this account represents the fiduciary's responsibility to the income beneficiaries. This Estate Income account will never have an opening balance. Nothing can appear in it until income is earned. Income and the expenses applicable to income are accumulated in the accounts listed in the 700 and 800 series during each accounting period, and these accounts are closed into Estate Income at the end of each period (usually annually)—just as the nominal accounts of any other business are closed into Investment or Surplus periodically. If distributions are made to income beneficiaries, account number 600, Distributions of Income, is debited. This account remains open until the final closing, but at any time, its balance, deducted from the balance in Estate Income, represents the undistributed income for which the fiduciary is accountable. This amount must be supported by the physical assets (frequently cash only) considered as belonging to Income—or the income beneficiaries.

Just as an ordinary investment account must always match the net assets of a business, so must the two fiduciary equity accounts always equal the fiduciary's net assets.

The Opening Bookkeeping Entry

The entry to open a fiduciary's set of books is simple—debit each proper account for whatever property is turned over to the executor or trustee (with a related credit for accompanying mortgages, if any) and credit Estate Principal (or Trust Principal) for the total.

But the determination of the pro per *amounts* to use in this entry is not always simple at all.

An Estate's Entry

For an estate, it is proper to use the valuations established by the appraisal as of the date of death, regardless of whether or not the alternate valuation date is used in filing the estate tax return. This is because the books are *fiduciary accounting* records, not tax records. Any necessary adjustments can always be made later for estate tax or income tax purposes.

In accounting for an estate, there is some difference of opinion as to whether or not "non-probate" property should be recorded on the books. This is property which does not go through probate under local law and for which the executor is not, therefore, responsible legally, but which must be considered for estate tax purposes. It includes such things as the survivor's portion of jointly held property paid for by the decedent, life insurance payable to a named beneficiary, and others. The treatment of such items is optional. The executor is responsible for their location, taxability, and control, and having them recorded on the books might be an aid to him in keeping control over them. On the other hand, for *strict* fiduciary accounting purposes, the executor has no responsibility or accountability for these items and they are not, therefore, proper inclusions in his accounting records.

As for community property, the entire value can be recorded with a contra account representing the surviving spouse's equity, or only the decedent's share can be shown. The first method is probably preferable because it provides more information while having no effect on the amount of the executor's accountability.

A Trust's Entry

In the case of an inter vivos trust, however, it must first be remembered that the transfer of property to the trust constitutes a gift, and the tax rules applicable to individual taxpayers may come into play. This means that, for tax purposes, the correct basis may not be known until many years after the gift was made; that is, if the property is sold at a gain, the grantor's basis would be used, if sold at a loss, the lower of the grantor's basis or fair market value at date of gift, and so on.

This makes an opening entry that will be correct in all cases for tax purposes an impossibility; but for *fiduciary accounting purposes,* it is general practice to record the property at its fair market value at the date of the transfer. And this is logical, because it is undoubtedly the present value of the property that the grantor has in mind when creating the trust; also, it is certainly the amount with which the trustee should be charged and be responsible for and upon which he should expect to produce income. If a later sale discloses that, for tax purposes, the valuation used in the opening entry was wrong, an adjustment will simply have to be made—for tax purposes.

Testamentary Trusts' Entries

One other possible situation exists—a testamentary trust. A testamentary trust is *created*—though not *activated*—at the time of the testator's death. The authority for its creation is the decedent's will, and its creation is legally established upon the probation of that will.

It is true that a trust cannot be a valid one unless it has property, but a testamentary trust is potentially in existence from the date of death and is, in effect, simply standing by and waiting to become valid and active whenever the estate executor decides to turn over all or any part of the trust property to the trustee. This may be a period of from several months to several years, but the trust entity is, and must be, legally ready to operate any time the executor makes that decision.

The testamentary trust has the *right* to property as of the date of its creator's death, but the property must first be held in administration and, in effect, in escrow by the executor for a period of time—time that is often needed before the executor can safely determine exactly what the trust property will consist of.

When the trustee receives the property he is receiving it *as of* the date of death, but his responsibility and accountability do not take effect until he has possession of the property; therefore, he should record the trust property at its value on the date of its transfer—that is the value he is charged with and the proper value for the measurement of his performance.

The same person may have been named to act as executor and as trustee. This person already has possession of the trust assets, so no formal, physical delivery is necessary, but in such cases his executorship records should be kept entirely distinct from his trusteeship records. The estate and the trust are two entirely separate entities, and the trusteeship cannot begin until the distribution of the property to the trustee is recorded on the executor's books.

Testamentary trusts are very common. As an example, suppose a testator died on January 1, 1982, and left all of his property to a charitable trust. He named the Citizens Bank and Trust Company as his executor and trustee. The bank served as estate executor and administered the estate for two years, settling and closing it on December 31, 1983. At that time, upon termination of the estate, all of the remaining property was turned over to the trustee, and the testamentary trust, which could not become activated until it received the property, went into effect. The bank's records as executor were closed out and a new set of books was established for the trusteeship. Although the same bank served in both capacities, there were two entirely separate fiduciaries involved and two entirely separate sets of books had to be kept.

Entries During Administration

Receipts and disbursements of cash are entered in the appropriate cash journal. All transactions not involving cash, such as the receipt or delivery of property, are entered in the general journal. An adequate explanation should follow each entry to identify the property involved and to enable the entry to be traced to its source.

The cash journals should be ruled off and posted to the general ledger as frequently as is needed to maintain adequate control. Except in very complex situations, this can be done at the end of the annual accounting period, but it is usually done monthly, or possibly quarterly or semi-annually. Each general journal entry is normally posted individually. Where subsidiary ledgers are maintained, they should be brought up to date frequently so that all necessary information can be readily extracted.

Business Income

It is possible, of course, for a proprietorship business to be one of the assets of a fiduciary, and the net income from this business becomes income to the fiduciary.

The accountant has the choice of incorporating the bookkeeping system of the business into the fiduciary's bookkeeping system or of continuing separate books for the business and using only a control account in the fiduciary books. Combining the two sets of books can cause numerous complications, so it is generally considered much more satisfactory to keep them separate.

One of the reasons that could be advanced for maintaining the books of an estate or trust on the accrual rather than the cash method is that the administration of the fund involves the running of a business for which the accrual method is appropriate. However, since the objectives of a commercial accounting system are different from those of a fiduciary accounting system and the account titles in the two systems are also basically dissimilar, it is usually advisable not to incorporate the books of the business in the fiduciary accounting system, especially if one is on the accrual basis and the other on the cash basis.

The business interest will have been given an appraised valuation, along with the other fiduciary assets, and it is this figure that will be debited to an asset account, Business Interest, on the fiduciary books. At the end of each accounting period of the business, the fiduciary will debit this asset account for the amount of the business net profit and will credit an income account for the same amount. As the fiduciary makes periodic withdrawals of cash from the business, the business interest account will be credited when the income cash account is debited on the fiduciary books.

If the business is a proprietorship and the fiduciary entity is an estate, the business books would have to be adjusted to reflect the appraised value of the property accounts at the decedent's death.

Assume that the decedent's proprietorship business consisted of the ownership and operation of an office building and that the depreciated value of the building was $150,000.00 and cash and other net assets were $10,000.00; the proprietor's investment account on the business books was $160,000.00. The business interest was appraised in the estate at $210,000.00, and that figure would be recorded on the fiduciary's books. An adjustment would be made to the business proprietorship investment account, increasing it by $50,000.00 to $210,000.00. The building would be adjusted to $200,000.00, its new stepped-up basis, and that is the figure on which future depreciation would be computed.

If the business is a corporation, none of the above would apply, of course. The corporate stock would simply be entered on the estate books at its appraised value and no adjustment would be necessary on the corporation's books.

Annual Closings and Final Closing

There are seldom any adjusting entries that need to be made at the end of each accounting period, because a fiduciary is usually on the cash basis and accruals are unnecessary. There will, however, be an entry to record depreciation if depreciation is to be considered an expense for fiduciary accounting purposes.

As for the annual closing entry, all of the income and expense accounts (700 and 800 series) are closed into the Income account. No other entries are necessary.

The final closing, upon termination, will consist of only three basic entries—an entry closing all income and expense accounts into the Income account, an entry closing Distributions of Income into the Income account, and one closing all of the accounts representing adjustments to and deductions from principal into the Principal account.

Theoretically, if all of the assets and earnings have been distributed to the beneficiaries, these three entries will result in the balancing of every account in the ledger.

Obviously, the closing entries for a fiduciary are almost identical with those for any other entity, the main difference, again, being the use of two proprietorship accounts instead of the usual one.

Summary

To summarize the main points to be kept in mind in designing the accounting system for a fiduciary:

1. The principal difference between a fiduciary's chart of accounts and that of a commercial business is that there are two different net worth accounts, one for principal and one for income. Each of these is accompanied by a distributions account, but these distributions accounts are very much the equivalent of a proprietorship drawing account.

2. In addition to a general ledger, a fiduciary's accounting system should include a general journal; subsidiary ledgers might be desirable; a combination cash receipts-disbursements book will suffice in most cases, or two or more separate journals can be used.

3. In designing any columnar journal for a fiduciary, two columns (debit and credit) must be provided for each cash account—Income Cash and Principal Cash—rather than the usual one pair of columns for each account.

4. In recording the assets of an estate it is customary to use the date of death valuations for each, even though the alternate date valuations might be used for tax purposes; for fiduciary accounting purposes it is the date of death valuations the executor is charged with and adjustments can be made later for estate tax and income tax purposes.

5. Assets transferred to a trust are recorded at their fair market values at the time of the transfer. This is logical because it is the present value of the property that the grantor has in mind when creating the trust and it is the amount with which the trustee should be charged and upon which he should expect to produce income.

6. Since fiduciary accounting records are almost invariably kept on the cash basis, accruals of any kind are very seldom necessary before closing the books.

7. The final closing usually requires only three basic entries—one closing all of the income and expense accounts into the Income account, one closing Distributions of Income into the Income account, and one closing all of the accounts representing adjustments to and deductions from Principal into the Principal account.

CHAPTER **Three**

The Fiduciary's Reports

3

The probate court is usually given complete jurisdiction over the administration of estates. It has the power to examine the accounts and vouchers of the executor or administrator and to consider and determine objections that may be made by interested parties in reference to the estate's administration. To accomplish this, the laws of all the states have provisions requiring the executor or administrator to file periodic accounting reports with the probate court.

As for a trust, a trustee had no common-law duty to file an inventory or other reports with the court, but some statutes have placed this obligation on some or all trustees. Many states now have comprehensive legislation governing the procedure on accountings. Generally, the trustee is required to account to the beneficiaries and the court at the time of termination of the trust, and he may be required to do so periodically during his administration. In some states, formal court accounting is required annually or at some other specified interval, whether the beneficiaries have requested it or not. In other states no periodic accounting is required but the trustee may submit accounts when he desires to do so, and he must submit them when requested by a qualified beneficiary.

Many corporate trustees voluntarily file annual accounts in court, even though they have not been required to do so by statute, court rule, or court decree. They present complete information regarding their administration while it is fresh and current and thereby, in most cases, secure a court decree approving their accounts, thus removing all doubts as to their liability for the administration to that point. This would seem to be advisable for individual trustees as well.

Since a person accepting the position of fiduciary usually subjects all of his actions in connection with the administration of the estate or trust to the review of the court, his knowledge that this is the case forces him to be more careful in complying with the governing statutes and the provisions of the will or trust instrument than he might be if he expected no such review. The effect of such a system is that it emphasizes to the fiduciary that his position is a position of trust, and it strengthens the possibility that he will faithfully accomplish the objectives of his administration.

The required reports are usually in the form of accounting statements, so the fiduciary accountant must be aware of the necessity of preparing these reports and of the type of reports appropriate for his fiduciary and in his particular jurisdiction.

Necessity for Periodic Reporting

The court does not actively supervise the day-to-day activities of any fiduciary. This would be manifestly impossible because there might be many estates and trusts in the process of administration within the jurisdiction of the court at any time.

The court's review and control are accomplished instead by the statutory requirements making it mandatory for a fiduciary to file with the court periodic reports and accountings of his stewardship. One of the first and most important duties of a fiduciary is to keep and render full and accurate accounts concerning the property in his hands. These reports, when filed and passed on by the court, become a matter of public record, which any interested parties may examine and to which they may file objections, if desired. The principal and income beneficiaries will also be interested in, and entitled to, copies of these reports.

The court also needs a report so that it can review the disbursements made by the fiduciary, for the purpose of determining whether the fiduciary is entitled to reimbursement for these expenditures. Theoretically, the fiduciary's expenditures are considered as having been made from his own personal funds but, if they are approved, he is reimbursed for them by being permitted to deduct them from the amount of the cash for which he is accountable. The court will permit him to be reimbursed for, or credited with, all proper claims against the property which he has paid and for all actual and necessary expenses incurred in good faith and with exercise of reasonable judgment in the care, management, and settlement of the estate or trust.

When Reports Are Required

Reports of the progress of the administration are made to the court as often as the fiduciary cares to make them, or upon order of the court, or as required by statute. If the administration is not completely settled at the end of the first year, the fiduciary is frequently required to make an accounting annually.

At the time of termination, a final report or accounting is always made. An exception to this requirement may sometimes be permitted if all the beneficiaries make and file an agreement with the court which makes the accounting unnecessary. Such a procedure is known as a settlement by "receipt and release," with the interested parties signifying by receipt and release that they have inspected the accounting and have received the property to which they are entitled, and consenting to the discharge of the executor, administrator, or trustee.

Interim Reports

Any report or accounting made to the court prior to final settlement is known as an interim report.

As suggested above, it is good practice for a fiduciary to prepare an interim report at the end of each year of the administration, even though he may not be required to do so. It is best to have the approval of the court, or to learn of any objections, periodically as the administration progresses rather than wait until too late.

Reports covering each twelve-month period from the date of the creation of the estate or trust are acceptable, but equally acceptable, and usually much easier to prepare, are reports covering periods corresponding to those covered by the fiduciary income tax returns; that is, the first report may include a period of less than a year (from the date of creation to the end of the first fiscal or calendar year), and each succeeding report will cover a full twelve-month period, except that the final report may again be for less than one year. Each report will cover an annual tax or accounting period, at which time any figures needed are easily available either in summary form or in detail; attempting to gather such information at some odd date in the middle of the accounting year is unnecessarily difficult.

The Final Report

The court might accept a final report covering only the period that has elapsed since the date of the most recent interim report, but a final report must generally include the entire period of administration—from the date of creation to the date of termination. This may cover a number of years, but its preparation should pose no particular problem if interim reports have been filed; such interim reports can easily be combined into a final, overall report.

The effect of a final accounting is to close the entity and discharge the fiduciary. The court will examine the final report and determine whether or not the various expenditures listed therein are proper charges for which the fiduciary may be reimbursed or credited. It will also hear and rule on any objections that may be raised by creditors or beneficiaries. If everything is in order, the court will then issue a decree of distribution and discharge the fiduciary and cancel his bond.

Form of Report

There is no uniformity whatsoever as to the proper form for an interim or final report. Most statutes have very little to say about just what kind of report shall be filed, frequently describing it in very general terms, such as "a statement of receipts and disbursements," but without specifying whether a detailed listing is required or whether a summary will suffice.

Each court is likely to have its own ideas about the format and content of a report. Some may insist on one certain form, others may accept any form that will present the information they need in making their review. It is advisable, therefore, for the accountant to find out from the judge or a lawyer about the court's requirements before spending time preparing a report that will not be acceptable to that court. (This will often be a frustrating experience for an accountant because many courts will insist on reports in a much less informative form than the accountant would otherwise normally prepare.)

Generally, however, a summary cash statement must be prepared, accompanied by detailed schedules of cash receipts and disbursements. Cancelled checks supporting the disbursements must often be presented to the court also. If the volume of transactions was very large, the detailed schedules might not be required, though the court might later ask for them if more detailed information is needed.

Features of a Report

A desirable feature of any fiduciary's report (though not always required by the court) is for it to show, in some way, the disposition of all property that came into the fiduciary's hands. The beginning inventory of property, plus gains and income and less losses, expenses, and distributions, should be shown to equal the closing list of property being held for final distribution or for management in subsequent periods.

Another desirable feature, of course, is for the report to show separately the estate's or trust's operating income and expenses rather than have them intermingled with receipts and disbursements having to do with the principal. It has been stressed earlier that principal and income should be carefully segregated in the accounts, and the fiduciary's report should take advantage of this segregation and make this very useful information available not only to the court but to both the principal beneficiaries and the income beneficiaries as well. Each will be interested in a report showing his particular part of the results of operations.

Charge and Discharge Statement

There is very little to guide the fiduciary or his lawyer or accountant in deciding on the best form for the reports, but it would seem that a "Charge and Discharge Statement," highly recommended for estate executors and trustees, would be the best form. This form will serve for either interim or final reports, and it seems to be acceptable to most courts.

A charge and discharge statement shows the fiduciary as being charged with all assets and funds that come under his control—the original assets, gains on sales, operating income, and so forth. There is deducted from this total the disbursements for which he claims credit—the losses on sales, operating expenses, distributions paid, and other expenditures. The balance is the amount with which the fiduciary is still charged, and it must be represented by cash and other assets still in his possession.

It is preferable to divide a charge and discharge statement into two parts. One should be a statement covering only items relating to the principal of the estate or trust, the other a statement covering only the income and the expenses against that income. Each will show a closing balance and the total of the two balances will agree with the amount of the current listing of net assets on hand.

To summarize, fiduciary reports might take any one of many different forms, depending on the legal requirements, the wishes of the governing court, and the size and nature of the estate or trust. The most simple kind of cash statement might suffice for a very small operation. For larger ones, more formal and more complex reports are desirable. But in any case, the charge and discharge statement recommended by most accounting writers is the most satisfactory type of report. Unfortunately, however, its use is still far from universal, due largely to the fact that many courts are unfamiliar with any accounting statement other than a cash receipts and disbursements statement, and insist on some less informative type of report.

Reports Illustrated

A simple cash receipts and disbursements statement, which might serve as an interim or a final report for a small estate, is shown in Figure 3-1. The same kind of statement could be used for a trust.

FIGURE 3-1

Estate of Walter Brown
Paul Adams, Executor

STATEMENT OF CASH RECEIPTS AND DISBURSEMENTS

For the Period December 18, 1981, to August 31, 1982

Cash on Hand and in Bank, December 18, 1981 $ 6,259.86

Receipts:

Dec. 26 - Collection of Accrued Salary	$ 900.00	
Dec. 30 - Rent on House	195.00	
Dec. 31 - Sale of Auto	4,200.00	
Jan. 15 - Rent on House	195.00	
Feb. 15 - Rent on House	195.00	
Feb. 28 - Proceeds from Sale of House	23,700.00	
Total Receipts		29,385.00
Total Cash Accountable		$35,644.86

Disbursements:

Dec. 21 - County Court Clerk, Probate Fees	$ 18.00	
Dec. 22 - County Judge, Probate Fee	22.50	
Dec. 27 - Bell Telephone Co., Debt	12.78	
Dec. 27 - Plaza Pharmacy, Debt	55.50	
Dec. 28 - Western Gas Company, Debt	29.91	
Dec. 28 - Electric Plant Board, Debt	16.35	
Dec. 31 - City Hospital, Debt	542.40	
Jan. 3 - Dr. Ralph Harvey, Debt	300.00	
Jan. 20 - George Wayne, Appraiser Fee	60.00	
Jan. 20 - Alan Mayer, Appraiser Fee	60.00	
Jan. 20 - Scott Vance, Appraiser Fee	60.00	
Jan. 21 - County Court Clerk, Filing Inventory	21.00	
Jan. 25 - White Funeral Home, Funeral Expenses	3,139.50	
Jan. 26 - Davis Furnace Co., Repairs to House	55.50	
Jan. 28 - First Presbyterian Church, Bequest	1,500.00	
Feb. 9 - Insurance Center, Insurance on House	53.64	
Feb. 27 - County Court Clerk, Stamps on Deed	26.40	
Mar. 3 - Frances Brown, Bequest	6,000.00	
Mar. 3 - John A. Brown, Bequest	6,000.00	
Apr. 14 - Internal Revenue Service, Debt	288.81	
Apr. 27 - Geo. Barner, Attorney, Deed and Title	127.50	
May 1 - Dept. of Revenue, Inheritance Tax	1,279.83	
June 15 - Geo. Barner, Attorney Fee	600.00	
Aug. 20 - Paul Adams, Executor Fee	2,400.00	
Aug. 28 - County Court Clerk, Settlement Fee	15.75	
Aug. 31 - County Judge, Settlement Fee	80.55	
Total Disbursements		22,765.92
Balance, Cash in Bank, August 31, 1982		$12,878.94

Although a report of this kind might be accepted by many courts, it really raises more questions than it answers, especially to an accountant. It makes no mention of the estate inventory, it furnishes no accounting for the inventoried assets, and so on. A much more informative report could be made as shown in Figure 3-2, with the foregoing statement of receipts and disbursements attached to it as a supporting schedule.

FIGURE 3-2

Estate of Walter Brown
Paul Adams, Executor

STATEMENT OF FINAL SETTLEMENT

For the Period December 18, 1981, to August 31, 1982

Assets per Inventory, December 18, 1981:		
Cash on Hand and in Bank	$ 6,259.86	
Residence, 1426 Lincoln Avenue	42,750.00	
Rental House, 416 Elm Street	23,400.00	
Salary Receivable	900.00	
Automobile	4,200.00	
Household Furnishings	2,400.00	
Total Assets		$79,909.86
Less: Inventory Value of Assets Sold or Realized:		
Rental House	$23,400.00	
Automobile	4,200.00	
Salary Receivable	900.00	28,500.00
Total Assets Not Sold		$51,409.86
Add: Cash Receipts, per Schedule		29,385.00
Total		$80,794.86
Deduct: Cash Disbursements, per Schedule		22,765.92
Estate Balance, August 31, 1982		$58,028.94
Balance Consisting of:		
Cash in Bank	$12,878.94	
Residence	42,750.00	
Household Furnishings	2,400.00	
Total Balance		$58,028.94

It should be noted that in order to combine a cash statement with what might be considered a fund balance statement it is necessary to eliminate from the inventory the value of any assets sold or realized, because these values are duplicated in the cash receipts.

If the beginning or closing inventories are very lengthy, they can be listed in separate schedules and only the totals shown on the statement.

The statement seen in Figure 3-2 with its supporting cash schedules adequately reports on the estate's administration and is a form that could be easily understood by most people. It still fails to show one important bit of information, however. It makes no distinction between transactions applying to the principal of the estate and those applicable to the estate's income. This can be corrected by making a segregation of the receipts and disbursements, in the body of the statement, as follows:

Add Cash Receipts, per Schedule:		
Principal Receipts	$28,800.00	
Receipts of Income	585.00	$29,385.00
Deduct Disbursements, per Schedule:		
Principal Disbursements	$22,656.78	
Disbursements of Income	109.14	$22,765.92

Although the above type of statement might be preferred by many courts, it is still a very poor substitute for the recommended charge and discharge statement. A charge and discharge statement not only lends itself to reporting on a large estate but also is adaptable to an estate of any size. As an illustration, the statement presented in Figure 3-3 is a typical charge and discharge statement, using the same small estate that was used in the preceding examples.

FIGURE 3-3

Estate of Walter Brown
Paul Adams, Executor

CHARGE AND DISCHARGE STATEMENT

For the Period December 18, 1981, to August 31, 1982

First as to Principal:

The Executor Charges Himself with:

Assets per Inventory (Schedule A)	$ 79,909.86	
Assets Subsequently Discovered (Schedule B)	—	
Gains on Realization of Assets (Schedule C)	146.10	$ 80,055.96

The Executor Credits Himself with:

Funeral and Administrative Expenses (Schedule D)	$	6,477.30	
Debts of Decedent Paid (Schedule E)		1,245.75	
Losses on Realization of Assets (Schedule F)		—	
Bequests Paid (Schedule G)		13,500.00	
State Inheritance Tax Paid		1,279.83	22,502.88
Leaving a Balance of Principal of			$ 57,553.08

Consisting of:

Cash in Bank	$ 12,403.08	
Residence	42,750.00	
Household Furnishings	2,400.00	
Total	$ 57,553.08	

Second as to Income:

The Executor Charges Himself with:

Rents Received			$ 585.00

The Executor Credits Himself with:

Repairs to Property	$	55.50	
Insurance on Rental Property		53.64	109.14
Leaving a Balance of Income of			$ 475.86

Consisting of:

Cash in Bank	$ 475.86

Schedule A—Assets per Inventory

Cash on Hand and in Bank	$ 6,259.86
Residence, 1426 Lincoln Avenue	42,750.00
Rental House, 416 Elm Street	23,400.00
Automobile	4,200.00
Salary Receivable	900.00
Household Furnishings	2,400.00
Total	$ 79,909.86

Schedule C—Gains on Realization of Assets

Proceeds, Sale of Rental House		$ 23,700.00
Less: Deed, Title, Stamps		153.90
Net Proceeds		$ 23,546.10
Inventory Value of House		23,400.00
Net Gain on Realization		$ 146.10

Schedule D—Funeral and Administrative Expenses

Funeral Expenses:			
White Funeral Home			$ 3,139.50
Administrative Expenses:			
County Court Clerk, Probate Fees	$	18.00	
County Judge, Probate Fees		22.50	
Appraisers' Fees		180.00	
County Court Clerk, Filing Fee		21.00	
George Barner, Attorney Fee		600.00	
Paul Adams, Executor Fee		2,400.00	
County Court Clerk, Settlement Fee		15.75	
County Judge, Settlement Fee		80.55	3,337.80
Total			$ 6,477.30

Schedule E—Debts of Decedent Paid

Bell Telephone Company	$	12.78
Plaza Pharmacy		55.50
Western Gas Company		29.91
Electric Plant Board		7.95
Troy Laundry		8.40
City Hospital		542.40
Dr. Ralph Harvey		300.00
Internal Revenue Service		288.81
Total		$ 1,245.75

Schedule G—Bequests Paid

First Presbyterian Church	$ 1,500.00
Frances Brown	6,000.00
John A. Brown	6,000.00
Total	$ 13,500.00

FIGURE 3-3 (continued)

A statement of this kind, with its supporting schedules, should satisfy any court's requirements and should give any income or principal beneficiary the information he desires.

Reference should be made to the chart of accounts given in Figure 2-1 and it will be seen how easily that set of accounts will lend itself to the preparation of a charge and discharge statement, whether it be for an interim statement or a final accounting.

A charge and discharge statement is always a cumulative statement covering the period from the inception of the entity to the current statement date. It is advisable for such a statement to be prepared at the time of each annual closing of the books, whether required or not, and if statements for some specific shorter period are needed they can easily be prepared from these annual statements.

Summary

The most important things for an accountant to keep in mind in preparing a fiduciary's reports are as follows:

1. There is no accepted standard form for a fiduciary's reports, as the requirements vary greatly from one jurisdiction to another.

2. Regardless of the exact form of a report, it is most desirable for it to show the disposition of all property that came into the fiduciary's hands, starting with the beginning inventory and ending with the closing inventory at the time of the report.

3. It is also desirable and almost mandatory for the report to divide the operations during the reporting period into two separate sections, one for the principal of the entity and one for its income.

4. A charge and discharge statement, with supporting schedules, is highly recommended as being the best form for an interim or a final report by an executor or a trustee.

CHAPTER **Four**

Accounting for an Estate

4

An estate in the process of administration is different from any other entity. It is even different in many ways from a trust, though there are many similarities between the two and both have the same general objectives and requirements.

The principles and rules of fiduciary accounting and reporting apply equally to both estates and trusts. Still, there are a few features peculiar to estate accounting, rather than to trusts, that should be pointed out, and these should serve as a reference for the estate accountant in planning the accounting system and in supervising the bookkeeping throughout the estate's administration.

Theory of Estate Accounting

The guiding principle in estate accounting is that there must be a proper segregation between principal transactions and income transactions.

The estate principal consists of all assets, including receivables, owned *as of the date of death.* These assets may change in form (as when cash is spent for securities) or even in amount (as when an asset is sold at a gain), but the estate's principal is still this group of assets. Transactions affecting the estate's income are all those generated by these principal assets *after the date of death.*

Just suppose that it would be possible to settle a decedent's estate completely on the same day the decedent died. All of his property would be assembled and converted to cash to whatever extent necessary, his debts would be paid, funeral and administrative expenses would be paid, death taxes would be paid, and legacies would be paid. All of these payments would, of course, be made out of the estate assets making up the principal, as there would be no other source of funds. There would be no estate income since no time would have elapsed during which income could have been earned. The remaining assets would be distributed to the proper beneficiaries and the estate would be settled.

A supposition of this kind is manifestly impossible, as some period of time is always needed to accomplish all of the necessary settlement actions. During this period, the estate would, presumably, be earning income; and there might be expenses against this income. These incomes and expenses originate and take place *after* the date of death, so they do not affect the estate's principal. They go to make up estate income.

State laws and common custom have, in effect, defined the charges against principal as those which would be necessary even if there were no income involved; everything else is charged to the estate's income. If the estate accountant keeps these principles in mind he should have little difficulty in handling an estate's accounting.

The Opening Entry

An inventory and appraisal of the estate assets is almost universally required by the probate laws. The executor must make a listing of every item of property owned by the decedent, and he is expected to be diligent in seeking out these items. Then, it is the duty of the one or more appraisers, appointed by the court, to determine the fair market value of each asset as of the date of the decedent's death. This inventory and appraisal establishes the amount of the executor's accountability and responsibility.

The estate inventory is always the basis for the opening entry in the estate's books, and this entry cannot be made until the inventory and appraisal is completed. This might cause a delay of several months, but in order to keep from getting far behind in the daily bookkeeping routine the journals may be started at once, delaying only their postings to the ledger until after the opening entry has been made and posted.

This opening entry will contain a number of debits—a debit for each asset shown on the inventory listing, after combining various items to fit into the asset accounts established in the general ledger chart of accounts. There will be only one credit entry, a credit to Estate Principal for the total amount of the estate as shown by the inventory. The inventory values are used in the books even though values at the later optional valuation date may be used for estate tax purposes.

No liabilities are included in an estate inventory, so none are entered on the estate books. However, as mentioned earlier, an existing long-term liability, such as a mortgage on an estate asset, can be recorded, with the debit being made to the Debts of Decedent account. This treatment is optional with the accountant.

Assets Not Inventoried

The executor might have difficulty in discovering all of the assets of a person who has died. If any such items are erroneously omitted from the estate inventory but later discovered by the executor, they must be entered in the estate books as soon as they are valued.

The credit side of this entry could be made to the Estate Principal account, as the amount of the executor's accountability has been increased, but it is considered better to credit, instead, the account Assets Not Inventoried. By handling the addition this way, the Estate Principal account will continue always to agree with the amount of the inventory originally filed with the court, and the amount of total accountability is the combined total of Estate Principal and Assets Not Inventoried.

Assets Not Inventoried will remain as an open account on the books during the entire life of the estate, and it will be closed into Estate Principal at the time of final closing of the books when the estate is terminated.

Debts of Decedent

Seldom does anyone die without owing debts of some kind, but these debts are not treated as liabilities on the estate books. They are, instead, handled on a strict cash basis, and when they are approved and paid they are charged to the account Debts of Decedent.

A decedent's debts existing at the time of his death might include such things as a utility bill, a doctor's account, other medical bills, income taxes due on the decedent's final (or previous) income tax returns, a note payable plus accrued interest, wages and salaries payable to employees, bills for purchases or services, property taxes due at the time of his death, checks written by the decedent but not paid by his bank before his death, and many others.

Care should be taken to prevent any of these debts existing at the time of death from being charged to expense accounts on the fiduciary books. They are of a different nature from expenses incurred in the operation of the estate after the decedent's death, as they are payable out of the estate's principal rather than from income; and they are payable from Principal Cash rather than from Income Cash.

The Debts of Decedent account is one of the several accounts that reduce the amount of the principal for which the executor is accountable, and this account remains open on the books until it is finally closed into Estate Principal upon termination of the estate.

Expenses Applicable to Principal

In addition to the decedent's debts, there are a number of other expenditures that are chargeable to the estate's principal rather than to its income, and that are in the nature of claims against the estate.

One of these is the expense of the decedent's funeral, and this includes not only the ordinary costs of burial but also a reasonable amount for flowers and the cost of a burial lot, a vault, monument, and tombstone.

Another is the expense of administering the estate. Included in this category are expenditures for the executor's fee, attorneys' and accountants' fees, court costs, filing fees, appraisers' fees, the defense of legal actions against the estate, and others. It is true that the executor has the option of deducting some of these payments as expense deductions on the estate's income tax return rather than as showing them as reductions in the gross estate on the estate tax return, but for *fiduciary accounting purposes* they must be shown as reductions in principal, never as expenses; they must be recorded in the contra-principal account for Administration Expenses.

The federal estate tax paid by an estate is also considered as being payable out of the principal of the estate, and it is charged to a separate account in the group of accounts representing deductions from Estate Principal; but although the federal tax is always payable out of the estate principal, the applicable statutes and the decedent's will must be consulted to determine whether the estate or the beneficiaries are liable for the payment of state inheritance taxes. If these are payable by the beneficiaries out of their shares of the estate, the executor can notify the various individuals of the amount of their liability and collect the proper amounts from each, but the most practical way of handling inheritance taxes is for the executor to pay these taxes and later withhold the payments from the distributions to the beneficiaries. In a great many cases, however, the decedent's will provides that such taxes shall be paid out of the general estate assets so that the various legacies may be paid in full without deductions; this is probably the best way, certainly the most simple, and the inheritance tax will be charged to the same account as the federal estate tax.

Gains and Losses on Realization

Another possible transaction that will affect the estate's principal is the realization of a gain or a loss on the disposition of an estate asset.

The values at which the estate assets are appraised and entered on the books are merely intelligent estimates, and it is very unlikely that the actual proceeds from the sale of any asset will be exactly the same as its book value.

An account is needed, therefore, for the recording of any gains or losses on the disposition of estate assets. An account called Gains and Losses on Realization should be included in the estate ledger. The nature of this account is that it represents a correction to the Estate Principal account, into which it will finally be closed. A credit balance in this account means that the executor has that much greater accountability than originally shown by Estate Principal; a debit balance means that he was charged with more value than was actually in the property. The Gains and Losses on Realization account will remain open during the life of the estate for the entering of corrections in inventory valuations disclosed by any sales up to the date of final settlement.

The term "gains and losses" as used here is unfortunate because it might be misleading. From a strict estate accounting standpoint, these gains and losses have nothing to do with income or expenses. As suggested earlier, they simply represent corrections in original valuations or an increase in the principal and do not enter into the computation of the estate's operating net income. If these entries were made directly to the Estate Principal account, their true nature would be clearer, but the books would not be so informative.

Gains and losses for income tax purposes are ignored at this point, so it must be remembered that, regardless of the tax treatment, only the Estate Principal, rather than Estate Income, is affected. For this reason, the Gains and Losses on Realization account will continue to be used even after filing the estate tax return, and any later taxable gains or losses can be picked up out of this account in preparing the estate's income tax returns, at which time the amount of the gain or loss will be adjusted, for tax purposes only, for the differences between the asset's book value and the correct tax basis.

Legacies and Distributions of Principal

Distribution of the estate's assets also, of course, reduces its principal.

Specific legacies provided for in the decedent's will are debited to the Legacies account when they are paid. Bequests of personal property other than cash are also charged to this account, and the asset account is credited, when the article is given to the named beneficiary.

Distributions of cash or other property out of the principal of the estate, whether made only at the time of final settlement or at various times during the life of the estate, are charged to the Distributions of Principal account.

The Legacies and Distributions accounts represent the portion of the executor's accountability that has been discharged. These accounts will finally total the same amount as shown in the Estate Principal account (reduced by the contra-principal accounts for debts, administrative expenses, and the like) which will mean that the executor has completely discharged his liability. Legacies and Distributions will then be closed into Estate Principal.

The Estate's Income and Expenses

Determination of the proper items that will make up the estate's income should pose no problem for the accountant. Nor should the expenses to be charged against that income be difficult to recognize. Transactions originating *after* the date of death, rather than *as of* the date of death, produce the estate's net income.

Earnings from all estate assets are applicable to income rather than to principal, regardless of whether the assets belong to principal or to income. Such earnings are those ordinarily thought of as being income—interest, rents, dividends, business profits, and others.

The expenses applicable to income are all those generally classed as ordinary operating expenses—office expense, repairs and maintenance, utilities, wages, property taxes, interest expense, travel, and so on.

The income items are credited to the proper accounts in the income section of the ledger, of course, and the expenses are charged to accounts in the expense section. These various accounts representing income and deductions from income would, if summarized into statement form, look very much like an ordinary profit and loss statement.

A slight difficulty might be encountered if a certain cash receipt includes both principal and income. For example, interest income accrued to the date of death is inventoried and is a part of the estate principal. The cash receipt in payment of this interest will also usually include interest from the date of death to the date of payment. In this case, debit Principal Cash for the accrued portion, debit Income Cash for the portion earned after death, credit the accrual for its amount, and credit Interest Income for the remainder.

Likewise, a single disbursement could include both elements. An example might be a check written in payment of a repairman's wages. The portion covering work performed prior to the decedent's death is a debit to Debts of Decedent, the remainder is a debit to Repairs Expense; Principal Cash is credited with the amount of the debt, Income Cash is credited with the balance.

Depreciation

Depreciation expense is also a charge against the estate's income (not always true with a trust), even though the depreciable assets belong to the estate principal.

Depreciable assets of an estate are subject to depreciation, and this must be provided for in the accounts. For estate accounting purposes, the depreciation basis for each asset is its newly acquired inventory valuation—the date of death value—regardless of its original cost or its book value at the date of death. The usual rules regarding asset life, salvage value, first year depreciation, and so on will be followed.

The decedent's will and local law should be studied carefully for any unusual instructions regarding depreciation. Sometimes these govern, to some extent, the proper treatment of depreciation in the accounts and particularly its proper income tax treatment. As a general rule, the income tax deduction for depreciation must be apportioned between the fiduciary and the income beneficiaries on the basis of income allocable to each, though this has no effect on the proper treatment of depreciation for fiduciary accounting purposes.

Income Taxes

There is one other common charge against an estate's income—the income taxes paid on the taxable income earned during the estate's administration.

Income taxes paid by the fiduciary on the estate's portion of the net earnings during administration are applicable to income rather than to principal; they represent a reduction in the amount for which the executor is accountable to the income beneficiaries.

It would not be improper to charge these income taxes directly to the Estate Income account, but income taxes are usually considered as a more direct reduction of the income to be distributed later to the income beneficiaries—more in the nature of an operating expense—and are charged to an account in the expense section of the ledger. As a result, the estate's net income, which is closed into Estate Income at the end of each accounting period, is the net income after income taxes.

A question arises as to the proper treatment of any portion of the income tax that might have been applicable to the taxable gains on realization described earlier. Should this part of the tax be a charge against principal rather than income? Technically, principal should be charged, but, as a matter of practice, this question is usually ignored unless the decedent's will or state law requires otherwise.

Income taxes paid by an executor in filing the decedent's final income tax return, as well as any taxes, penalties, and interest due on prior years, are not subject to the above rules. Such taxes were liabilities of the decedent at the time of death and are simply charged to the Debts of Decedent account on the estate books.

Summary

The special features of estate accounting are as follows:

1. The situation in effect at the date of death governs the segregation of principal and income of an estate.

2. The basis for everything that takes place in estate accounting is the inventory and appraisal required by law.

3. The original inventory and appraisal might have to be amended if additional estate assets are discovered.

4. Certain payments are made by estates but not by other fiduciaries. These include the decedent's debts, funeral expenses, appraisers' fees, legacies, and death taxes, and they are charges against principal.

5. All income and expenses generated by the estate assets after the date of death constitute the estate's income.

CHAPTER Five

Case Study in Estate Accounting

5

Many of the principles and procedures described earlier might best be illustrated by a detailed study of the accounting for a rather typical, medium-to-large-sized estate.

The decedent in this case was George Webb, who died on January 2, 1982, at the age of fifty-nine. Mr. Webb died testate, his will naming Bruce Jackson as his executor.

Mr. Webb was the owner of a successful retail business, but had amassed a large part of his fortune over the years from local rental property, from buying and selling such property, and by investing in real estate, real estate mortgages, and securities.

His will was relatively simple. It provided that his diamond ring should be given to his brother, that a bequest of $5,000.00 be given to his church, and that his proprietorship business be left in trust to his son, age 26, until the son becomes 31 years of age, at which time it shall go to the son outright; the First National Bank was named as trustee of this trust. The automobiles, household furnishings, and other jewelry are to be given to Mrs. Webb.

The remainder of his estate, after the above bequests and after the payment of taxes and expenses, is to be given to his widow. Mr. Webb also provided that his executor shall distribute the sum of $1,500.00 per month to the widow during the period of the estate's administration.

The will also provided that all estate and inheritance taxes should be paid by his estate rather than by any individual beneficiaries.

The Estate Inventory

After qualifying as executor, Bruce Jackson spent several days locating and listing all of the decedent's assets. He then called on the court-appointed appraisers to evaluate the various items, and this job was completed on January 28, 1982.

The inventory and appraisal, a copy of which was filed with the probate court, was as shown in Figure 5-1.

FIGURE 5-1

Cash on Hand	$ 470.60
Cash in Bank	18,275.90
Residence, Owned Jointly with	
Wife with Survivorship, but	
Paid for Entirely by Decedent	85,000.00
Life Insurance, Payable to Wife	
as Named Beneficiary	100,000.00
Proprietorship Business	200,000.00
Real Estate Mortgages Receivable	726,421.75
Interest Receivable on Mortgages	2,724.08
Corporate Stocks	178,322.40
Municipal Bonds	118,408.85
Accrued Interest on Bonds	1,628.10
Rental Building	120,000.00
Accrued Rents on Building	1,300.00
Diamond Ring	6,000.00
Other Jewelry	3,500.00
Household Furnishings	12,000.00
Automobiles	8,450.00
Director Fee Receivable	250.00
Total Gross Estate	$1,582,751.68

The executor discovered that Mr. Webb had made only one lifetime gift, a gift of $25,000.00 in cash to his son on July 2, 1981. A gift tax return had been filed for this gift, but no gift tax was payable on it. Although this gift might have to be considered for estate tax purposes, it had no effect on the probate estate, the executor had no responsibility in connection with it, and it was not accountable in any way, so it was properly omitted from the estate inventory.

The residence and the life insurance were not a part of the legal, or probate, estate, but the executor was not aware of this at the time; they were included for the sake of completeness and no harm was done by this.

The Bookkeeping System

The estate's accountant, using the inventory as a guide and trying to foresee the type and probable volume of transactions that might be expected during the administration, planned the bookkeeping system for the fiduciary. His first step was the preparation of a chart of accounts for the general ledger (Figure 5-2).

FIGURE 5-2

CHART OF ACCOUNTS

100 - Cash on Hand
101 - Principal Cash
102 - Income Cash
103 -
104 - Business Interest
105 - Mortgages Receivable
106 - Interest Receivable on Mortgages
107 - Corporate Stocks
108 - Municipal Bonds
109 - Accrued Interest on Bonds
110 -
111 - Rental Building
112 - Accrued Rents on Building
113 - Allowance for Depreciation
114 - Diamond Ring
115 - Other Jewelry
116 - Household Furnishings
117 - Automobiles
118 - Directors Fee Receivable
119 -
120 -
121 -

200 -
201 -

300 - Estate Principal
301 - Assets Not Inventoried
401 - Debts of Decedent
402 - Funeral Expenses
403 - Administration Expenses
404 - Estate and Inheritance Taxes
405 - Gains and Losses on Realization
406 - Legacies Paid
407 - Distributions of Principal

500 - Estate Income
600 - Distributions of Income

700 - Business Income
701 - Interest on Mortgages
702 - Dividends Received
703 - Interest on Municipal Bonds
704 - Rental Income
705 -
706 -
707 -

800 - Office Expenses
801 - Building Repairs
802 - Insurance
803 - Utilities
804 - Real Estate Taxes
805 - Depreciation
806 - Interest Expense
807 - Income Taxes Paid
808 -
809 -
810 -
811 -
812 -

It was very possible, even likely, that other accounts might need to be added later as the administration progressed, but these were all that could be foreseen at the time.

In addition to the general ledger, of course, a general journal was provided.

Also, three subsidiary ledgers were needed—one for the thirty-eight real estate mortgages making up the total shown on the inventory, one for the sixteen different corporate stocks included, and one for twelve issues of municipal bonds.

As for journals, although a rather large number of transactions could be anticipated in the collections on the mortgages and in receipts of dividends and bond interest, the accountant decided that a combination cash receipts and disbursements journal would suffice; if this proved impractical, a change could easily be made to two separate journals, for receipts and for disbursements. Column headings for this journal were as seen in Figure 5-3.

FIGURE 5-3

Date
Payee or Explanation
Check or Receipt Number

Dr. Principal Cash, No. 101
Cr. Principal Cash, No. 101
Dr. Income Cash, No. 102
Cr. Income Cash, No. 102
Cr. Mortgages Receivable, No. 105
Cr. Interest on Mortgages, No. 701
Cr. Dividends Received, No. 702
Cr. Interest on Municipal Bonds, No. 703
Cr. Rental Income, No. 704
Dr. Debts of Decedent, No. 401
Dr. Funeral Expenses, No. 403
Dr. Administration Expenses, No. 403
Dr. Estate, Inheritance Taxes, No. 404
Dr. Office Expenses, No. 800
Dr. Building Repairs, No. 801
Dr. Insurance, No. 802
Dr. Utilities, No. 803
Dr. Real Estate Taxes, No. 804
Dr. Income Taxes Paid, No. 807

Other Accounts - Account Number
Other Accounts - Debit
Other Accounts - Credit

The Opening Entry

The bookkeeping system could not actually be set up until the completion of the inventory and appraisal on January 28, 1982, but in the meantime a record of each cash receipt was kept in a duplicate receipt book and the disbursements were, of course, recorded in the check stubs. These were later entered into the journal.

The opening entry, which was recorded in the general journal, was as shown in Figure 5-4.

FIGURE 5-4

100	Cash on Hand	470.60	
101	Principal Cash	18,275.90	
104	Business Interest	200,000.00	
105	Mortgages Receivable	726,421.75	
106	Interest Receivable	2,724.08	
107	Corporate Stocks	178,322.40	
108	Municipal Bonds	118,408.85	
109	Accrued Interest on Bonds	1,628.10	
111	Rental Building	120,000.00	
112	Accrued Rents on Building	1,300.00	
114	Diamond Ring	6,000.00	
115	Other Jewelry	3,500.00	
116	Household Furnishings	12,000.00	
117	Automobiles	8,450.00	
118	Director Fee Receivable	250.00	
300	Estate Principal		1,397,751.68

It should be noted that the residence was not included in the opening entry. As mentioned before, this asset was owned jointly with the wife with survivorship and passed directly to her outside of the will. It was not a part of the probate property, so the executor was not responsible for it and it was not a proper part of the opening entry. (This treatment is optional, however; some executors might choose to include such property in order to have the bookkeeping record of it which they will need for estate tax purposes.) The same is true with the life insurance, which goes directly to the widow; it should not be recorded.

Transactions for the Year 1982

The fiduciary's transactions for the year 1982 are given below. Most of the entries for these were made in the cash journal, but they are given here in general journal form, along with the ledger account numbers to which they would be posted.

1. The cash on hand of $470.60 was deposited into the estate's bank account.

101	Principal Cash	470.60	
100	Cash on Hand		470.60

    It is seldom necessary to have cash on hand, unless a petty cash or working fund is found to be needed. All cash should be deposited in the bank account.

2. The executor paid $200.00 in probate fees and costs to the probate judge and the clerk of the probate court.

403	Administration Expenses	200.00	
101	Principal Cash		200.00

    Such fees are, of course, proper charges against the principal of the estate.

3. The director fees of $250.00 receivable by the decedent at the time of his death were collected in January 1982.

101	Principal Cash	250.00	
118	Director Fee Receivable		250.00

    These fees are "Income in Respect of a Decedent," accrued income at the date of death, as are the interest on the mortgages and bonds up to the date of death and the accrued rental income. There would also be included in this category declared dividends, the record date of which is prior to the date of death. When these items are collected, the asset account must be written off the books but no income is recorded; still, they must later be shown as income for income tax purposes, so it is necessary to make memorandum records of this income for later use in preparing the fiduciary's tax return.

4. On February 20, 1982, the executor paid for the decedent's funeral expenses in the amount of $2,000.00; also for a burial plot costing $500.00 and a headstone costing $400.00.

402	Funeral Expenses	2,900.00	
101	Principal Cash		2,900.00

    Not only the actual funeral expenses but also the cost of a burial plot and a suitable monument are proper charges against the estate's principal.

5. On February 21, 1982, the executor gave the diamond ring to Mr. Webb's brother, as directed in the will.

406	Legacies Paid	6,000.00	
114	Diamond Ring		6,000.00

    This legacy represents a partial distribution of the principal of the estate, and this charge to the Legacies account reduces the amount for which the executor is responsible.

6. On March 1, 1982, the executor discovered that Mr. Webb had another bank account which had not been known about previously. The amount of this deposit was $10,000.00.

101	Principal Cash	10,000.00	
301	Assets Not Inventoried		10,000.00

The money in the new account was deposited into the estate's bank account. The credit side of this entry could have been made directly to the Estate Principal account, but it is usually considered better to leave that account always with its original balance and to use other accounts to show any changes in principal.

7. Mr. Webb was liable on a note payable to the Commercial Bank in the amount of $5,000.00. This note became due on March 31, 1982, and the executor paid it plus $475.00 of interest. One half of that interest had accrued up to the time of Mr. Webb's death; the balance was for the period after death.

401	Debts of Decedent	5,237.50	
806	Interest Expense	237.50	
101	Principal Cash		5,237.50
102	Income Cash		237.50

The interest which was payable at the date of the decedent's death is known as a "Deduction in Respect of Decedent." An item of this kind is deductible both for estate tax purposes and for fiduciary income tax purposes, so some record should be made so that it will not be overlooked for both tax returns.

8. The decedent's debts existing at the time of his death, for doctors' bills, drug bills, telephone, and others, amounted to $897.00. These were paid by the executor in March 1982.

401	Debts of Decedent	897.00	
101	Principal Cash		897.00

All such liabilities existing at the time of death are simply handled on a cash basis, and they are proper charges against principal.

9. The estate's accountant prepared Mr. Webb's individual income tax return for the year 1981 and determined that a balance of $1,437.50 was due on this return. The executor filed the return and paid the tax on April 1, 1982.

401	Debts of Decedent	1,437.50	
101	Principal Cash		1,437.50

This is another liability that existed at the time of death, so it should be paid from principal cash and is a proper charge against the principal of the estate.

10. In order to raise cash for the payment of estate taxes, the executor sold some of the mortgages, having a book value of $192,475.20, for $183,982.10—a loss of $8,493.10.

101	Principal Cash	183,982.10	
405	Gains, Losses on Realization	8,493.10	
105	Mortgages Receivable		192,475.20

Although this loss on realization may be a deduction for income tax purposes, from a fiduciary accounting standpoint it is simply an adjustment to the original valuation of the total estate and has no relation to income or expense. Theoretically, some of the mortgages sold were simply not worth their face value.

11. The executor also sold some of the corporate stocks, with a book value of $36,928.50, for $39,816.21, making a gain of $2,887.71.

101	Principal Cash	39,816.21	
107	Corporate Stocks		36,928.50
405	Gains, Losses on Realization		2,887.71

If these stocks sold were listed stocks, their date of death valuation was not just an estimate but an accurate figure; still, their sale at a gain does not produce estate income but is an adjustment to the amount of the estate's principal. This is because the assets may change in form, *or even in amount,* but still constitute the principal of the estate. The effect, then, is just the same as in the preceding transaction.

12. In September 1982 the executor filed the federal estate tax return with a payment of $235,800.00 and the state inheritance tax return with a payment of $20,883.00.

| 404 | Estate and Inheritance Taxes | 256,683.00 | |
| 101 | Principal Cash | | 256,683.00 |

13. The executor gave Mr. Webb's church a check for $5,000.00 as directed by the will.

| 406 | Legacies Paid | 5,000.00 | |
| 101 | Principal Cash | | 5,000.00 |

Again, the legacies account really represents a partial distribution of the principal of the estate, a discharge of a part of the executor's accountability to the principal beneficiaries, of which the church is one.

14. By November 25, 1982, the estate's cash had accumulated enough through collections, sales of assets, and so on, to warrant its investment, so the executor bought $100,000.00 in government bonds, $20,000.00 of this coming from principal cash and $80,000.00 from income cash.

119	Government Bonds	100,000.00	
101	Principal Cash		20,000.00
102	Income Cash		80,000.00

This necessitates a new account in the ledger, "Government Bonds," which had not been foreseen earlier.

15. Collections on the mortgages during the year totalled $115,377.95, of which
$65,377.95 was for interest and $50,000.00 was on principal.

101	Principal Cash	52,724.08	
102	Income Cash	62,653.87	
106	Interest Receivable		2,724.08
105	Mortgages Receivable		50,000.00
701	Interest on Mortgages		62,653.87

The interest receivable at the date of death was included in the interest collections, so that much of these collections is a part of the principal of the estate and becomes Principal Cash with the receivable being written off. The remainder of the interest received is income to the fiduciary.

16. Dividends received on the corporate stocks during the year 1982 amounted to
$8,916.12.

102	Income Cash	8,916.12	
702	Dividends Received		8,916.12

17. Interest collected on the municipal bonds during the year was $5,920.44.

101	Principal Cash	1,628.10	
102	Income Cash	4,292.34	
109	Accrued Interest on Bonds		1,628.10
703	Interest on Municipal Bonds		4,292.34

The accrued portion of this interest is also Income in Respect of a Decedent, but it can be ignored as taxable income in this case since it is from municipal bonds.

18. Building rentals collected during the year were $14,400.00.

101	Principal Cash	1,300.00	
102	Income Cash	13,100.00	
112	Accrued Rents on Building		1,300.00
704	Rental Income		13,100.00

Again, a portion of the collection had been included in the inventory and must be written off; the remainder, the portion accruing after the date of death, is income.

19. At the end of the year 1982 the income statement for the proprietorship business showed that a net profit of $32,000.00 had been earned. During the year the executor had drawn cash from the business from time to time in the total amount of $32,000.00

104	Business Interest	32,000.00	
700	Business Income		32,000.00
102	Income Cash	32,000.00	
104	Business Interest		32,000.00

It would be rather unusual for the cash withdrawals from the business to match exactly the business net profit, but assume that it happened in this case.

20. Expenses in connection with the rental building during the year were $900.00 for taxes, $750.00 for insurance, $1,120.00 for repairs, and $2,300.00 for utilities—a total of $5,070.00.

801	Repairs	1,120.00	
802	Insurance	750.00	
803	Utilities	2,300.00	
804	Taxes, Real Estate	900.00	
102	Income Cash		5,070.00

These items are a proper and typical charge against the income of the estate rather than against its principal.

21. The executor, in accordance with the terms of the will, distributed $1,500.00 per month of the estate earnings to Mrs. Webb.

| 600 | Distributions of Income | 18,000.00 | |
| 102 | Income Cash | | 18,000.00 |

This represents a partial discharge of the amount for which the executor is responsible to the income beneficiary.

22. Clerk hire and office expenses incurred in the operation of the estate during the year amounted to $9,200.00.

| 800 | Office Expenses | 9,200.00 | |
| 102 | Income Cash | | 9,200.00 |

It might be thought that expenses of this kind are administration expenses and, therefore, a deduction from principal rather than from income, but these expenses are really more necessary in handling the collections, payments of expenses, and the daily routine of operating the estate than in its actual administration and are generally considered as proper charges against income.

23. A partial payment on the estate attorney's fee was made in the amount of $10,000.00 and a partial payment to the estate's accountant was made for $3,000.00.

| 403 | Administration Expenses | 13,000.00 | |
| 101 | Principal Cash | | 13,000.00 |

24. Depreciation on the rental building for the year was $3,600.00.

| 805 | Depreciation Expense | 3,600.00 | |
| 113 | Allowance for Depreciation | | 3,600.00 |

An allowance for depreciation is proper, and it is an operating expense rather than a reduction in principal.

Closing Entries for the Year

Preparatory to closing the estate books at the end of 1982 and preparing the year-end, interim report to the court, the estate's accountant extracted the trial balance shown in Figure 5-5, from the estate ledger:

FIGURE 5-5

		Debit	Credit
101	Principal Cash	3,091.99	
102	Income Cash	8,454.83	
104	Business Interest	200,000.00	
105	Mortgages Receivable	483,946.55	
107	Corporate Stocks	141,393.90	
108	Municipal Bonds	118,408.85	
111	Rental Building	120,000.00	
113	Allowance for Depreciation		3,600.00
115	Other Jewelry	3,500.00	
116	Household Furnishings	12,000.00	
117	Automobiles	8,450.00	
119	Government Bonds	100,000.00	
300	Estate Principal		1,397,751.68
301	Assets Not Inventoried		10,000.00
401	Debts of Decedent	7,572.00	
402	Funeral Expenses	2,900.00	
403	Administration Expenses	13,200.00	
404	Estate and Inheritance Taxes	256,683.00	
405	Gains, Losses on Realization	5,605.39	
406	Legacies Paid	11,000.00	
600	Distributions of Income	18,000.00	
700	Business Income		32,000.00
701	Interest on Mortgages		62,653.87
702	Dividends Received		8,916.12
703	Interest on Municipal Bonds		4,292.34
704	Rental Income		13,100.00
800	Office Expenses	9,200.00	
801	Building Repairs	1,120.00	
802	Insurance	750.00	
803	Utilities	2,300.00	
804	Real Estate Taxes	900.00	
805	Depreciation	3,600.00	
806	Interest Expense	237.50	
		$ 1,532,314.01	$ 1,532,314.01

No adjusting journal entries are necessary. The only entry needed for this annual closing is one closing all of the income and expense accounts into Estate Income, as in Figure 5-6.

FIGURE 5-6

700	Business Income	32,000.00	
701	Interest on Mortgages	62,653.87	
702	Dividends Received	8,916.12	
703	Interest on Municipal Bonds	4,292.34	
704	Rental Income	13,100.00	
800	Office Expenses		9,200.00
801	Building Repairs		1,120.00
802	Insurance		750.00
803	Utilities		2,300.00
804	Real Estate Taxes		900.00
805	Depreciation		3,600.00
806	Interest Expense		237.50
500	Estate Income		102,854.83

Interim Report to the Court

The accountant then prepared the Charge and Discharge Statement shown in Figure 5-7, supported by the schedules mentioned in the body of the report, for presentation to the court and to the beneficiaries.

The preparation of a report of this kind is really very easy if the books have been kept in the way they were in this case. Almost everything needed can be picked up from the trial balance.

FIGURE 5-7

Estate of George Webb
Bruce Jackson, Executor

CHARGE AND DISCHARGE STATEMENT

For the Period January 1, 1982, to December 31, 1982

First as to Principal:

The Executor Charges Himself with:

Assets per Inventory (Schedule A)	$ 1,397,751.68	
Assets Not Inventoried (Schedule B)	10,000.00	$ 1,407,751.68

The Executor Credits Himself with:

Funeral Expenses (Schedule C)	$ 2,900.00	
Debts of Decedent (Schedule D)	7,572.00	
Administration Expenses (Schedule E)	13,200.00	
Gains, Losses on Realization (Schedule F)	5,605.39	
Legacies Paid (Schedule G)	11,000.00	
Estate and Inheritance Taxes	256,683.00	296,960.39
Leaving a Balance of Principal of		$ 1,110,791.29

Consisting of:

Cash in Bank	$ 3,091.99
Business Interest	200,000.00
Mortgages	483,946.55
Corporate Stocks	141,393.90
Municipal Bonds	118,408.85
Rental Building (Net)	116,400.00
Other Jewelry	3,500.00
Household Furnishings	12,000.00
Automobiles	8,450.00
Government Bonds (Part)	23,600.00
	$ 1,110,791.29

Second as to Income:

The Executor Charges Himself with:

Business Income	$ 32,000.00	
Interest on Mortgages	62,653.87	
Dividends Received	8,916.12	
Interest on Municipal Bonds	4,292.34	
Rental Income	13,100.00	$ 120,962.33

(continued)

The Executor Credits Himself with:

Office Expenses		$ 9,200.00	
Building Repairs		1,120.00	
Insurance		750.00	
Utilities		2,300.00	
Real Estate Taxes		900.00	
Depreciation		3,600.00	
Interest Expense		237.50	
Distribution of Income		18,000.00	36,107.50
Leaving a Balance of Income of			$ 84,854.83

Consisting of:

Cash in Bank	$	8,454.83
Government Bonds (Part)		76,400.00
	$	84,854.83

FIGURE 5-7 (continued)

Transactions for the Year 1983

The executor set a target date of December 31, 1983, for completing the administration of this estate, believing that by that time he would have clearance on all taxes and that all other phases of the operations would be completed.

Following are the transactions for the year 1983, given in general journal form.

1. On January 1, 1983, the executor turned the entire operation of the proprietorship business over to the trustee for Mr. Webb's son.

407	Distributions of Principal	200,000.00	
104	Business Interest		200,000.00

   When a will provides for a trust to be established, it is best to turn the assets over to that trust as soon as practicable so that the income on those assets will not be superimposed on the fiduciary's already large income and be taxed at a higher bracket than if taxed to the trust or its beneficiaries.

2. The executor turned over the automobiles, jewelry, and household furnishings to the widow, as directed by the will. (The widow had actually had possession and use of these items since the date of death; this entry just formalizes the transaction.)

407	Distributions of Principal	23,950.00	
117	Automobiles		8,450.00
116	Household Furnishings		12,000.00
115	Other Jewelry		3,500.00

This, again, is a partial distribution of the principal of the estate.

3. The estate accountant computed the fiduciary's income tax for the year 1982 on Form 1041 and found that the tax due was $40,732.00. The executor filed this form and paid the tax on April 5, 1983.

807	Income Taxes Paid	40,732.00	
102	Income Cash		40,732.00

The estate accountant and the executor did a very poor bit of post-mortem estate planning in this case. An executor always has the option of deducting estate administration expenses either as a deduction from gross estate on the estate tax return or as an expense deduction on the fiduciary income tax return. In this case, the income tax bracket on the estate's large income was very much higher than the top bracket for estate taxation. The executor used all of the administration expenses on the estate tax return, but it would have been very much better if he had withheld all, or at least a part, of them from that return and used them to reduce the taxable income of the estate. A large tax saving would have been effected. Also, he would have been wise to elect a fiscal year ending on, say, June 30, 1982, rather than a calendar year which had to include a full twelve months of income. When the income of an estate is as large as it was in this case, it certainly makes sense to do everything possible to have it taxed in as low a bracket as possible.

4. The executor collected $43,555.00 of interest and $30,036.00 on the principal of the remaining mortgages during the year 1983.

102	Income Cash	43,555.00	
101	Principal Cash	30,036.00	
701	Interest on Mortgages		43,555.00
105	Mortgages Receivable		30,036.00

5. Dividends collected during the year amounted to $7,804.16.

102	Income Cash	7,804.16	
702	Dividends Received		7,804.16

6. Interest collected on the municipal bonds was $4,292.34.

102	Income Cash	4,292.34	
703	Interest on Municipal Bonds		4,292.34

7. Rental income from the building during the year amounted to $14,400.00.

102	Income Cash	14,400.00	
704	Rental Income		14,400.00

8. Toward the end of the year cash was needed for the payment of fees and ex-

penses, so the executor cashed $50,000.00 of the government bonds, placing $40,000.00 of this in principal cash, the remainder in income cash.

101	Principal Cash	40,000.00	
102	Income Cash	10,000.00	
119	Government Bonds		50,000.00

9. Interest collected on the government bonds during the year amounted to $5,500.00.

102	Income Cash	5,500.00	
706	Interest on Government Bonds		5,500.00

10. Building repairs for the year were $1,860.00, insurance was $790.00, real estate taxes $1,050.00, and utilities $2,400.00—a total of $6,100.00.

801	Building Repairs	1,860.00	
802	Insurance	790.00	
803	Utilities	2,400.00	
804	Real Estate Taxes	1,050.00	
102	Income Cash		6,100.00

11. Clerk hire and other office expenses amounted to $9,500.00 for the year.

800	Office Expenses	9,500.00	
102	Income Cash		9,500.00

12. Distributions of $1,500.00 per month were made to Mrs. Webb in 1983.

600	Distributions of Income	18,000.00	
102	Income Cash		18,000.00

13. In December the executor paid the remainder of the fees due to the estate's attorney and accountant, amounting to $12,000.00.

403	Administration Expenses	12,000.00	
101	Principal Cash		12,000.00

14. The executor's fee for administering this estate was set by the court, based on state law, in the amount of $50,000.00. The executor wrote himself a check for this amount.

403	Administration Expenses	50,000.00	
101	Principal Cash		50,000.00

15. The accountant was able to determine the fiduciary's taxable income just before the end of the year and found that the income tax for 1983 would be $14,942.00. A check was written for this amount, to be sent in with the Form 1041 later.

807	Income Taxes Paid	14,942.00	
102	Income Cash		14,942.00

Here, again, it might have been better to use some of the administration expenses as a deduction against this year's income rather than as an estate tax deduction.

16. Fees and costs for closing the estate were determined to be $680.00 and checks were written to cover them.

| 403 | Administration Expenses | 680.00 | |
| 101 | Principal Cash | | 680.00 |

17. Depreciation on the rental building for the year amounted to $3,600.00.

| 805 | Depreciation | 3,600.00 | |
| 113 | Allowance for Depreciation | | 3,600.00 |

Closing Entries for the Year

The accountant prepared the trial balance of the ledger as of December 31, 1983, as seen in Figure 5-8.

FIGURE 5-8

		Debit	Credit
101	Principal Cash	10,447.99	
102	Income Cash	4,732.33	
105	Mortgages Receivable	453,910.55	
107	Corporate Stocks	141,393.90	
108	Municipal Bonds	118,408.85	
111	Rental Building	120,000.00	
113	Allowance for Depreciation		7,200.00
119	Government Bonds	50,000.00	
300	Estate Principal		1,397,751.68
301	Assets Not Inventoried		10,000.00
401	Debts of Decedent	7,572.00	
402	Funeral Expenses	2,900.00	
403	Administration Expenses	75,880.00	
404	Estate and Inheritance Taxes	256,683.00	
405	Gains, Losses on Realization	5,605.39	
406	Legacies Paid	11,000.00	
407	Distributions of Principal	223,950.00	
500	Estate Income		102,854.83
600	Distributions of Income	36,000.00	
701	Interest on Mortgages		43,555.00
702	Dividends Received		7,804.16
703	Interest on Municipal Bonds		4,292.34
704	Rental Income		14,400.00
706	Interest on Government Bonds		5,500.00
800	Office Expenses	9,500.00	
801	Building Repairs	1,860.00	
802	Insurance	790.00	
803	Utilities	2,400.00	
804	Real Estate Taxes	1,050.00	
805	Depreciation	3,600.00	
807	Income Taxes Paid	55,674.00	
		1,593,358.01	1,593,358.01

The closing entries at this point will be the same as for any other annual closing, as in Figure 5-9.

FIGURE 5-9

701	Interest on Mortgages	43,555.00	
702	Dividends Received	7,804.16	
703	Interest on Municipal Bonds	4,292.34	
704	Rental Income	14,400.00	
706	Interest on Government Bonds	5,500.00	
800	Office Expenses		9,500.00
801	Building Repairs		1,860.00
802	Insurance		790.00
803	Utilities		2,400.00
804	Real Estate Taxes		1,050.00
805	Depreciation		3,600.00
807	Income Taxes Paid		55,674.00
500	Estate Income		677.50

Final Report to the Court

In order to terminate the administration as of December 31, 1983, the executor had to present an accounting of his administration to the court for approval. The accountant prepared the Charge and Discharge Statement shown in Figure 5-10, covering the entire two-year period of administration.

FIGURE 5-10

Estate of George Webb
Bruce Jackson, Executor

CHARGE AND DISCHARGE STATEMENT

For the Period January 2, 1982, to December 31, 1983

First as to Principal:

The Executor Charges Himself With:

Assets Per Inventory (Schedule A)	$ 1,397,751.68	
Assets Not Inventoried (Schedule B)	10,000.00	$ 1,407,751.68

The Executor Credits Himself With:

Funeral Expenses (Schedule C)	$ 2,900.00	
Debts of Decedent (Schedule D)	7,572.00	
Administration Expenses (Schedule E)	75,880.00	
Gains, Losses on Realization (Schedule F)	5,605.39	
Legacies Paid (Schedule G)	11,000.00	
Estate and Inheritance Taxes Paid	256,683.00	
Distributions of Principal	223,950.00	583,590.39
Leaving a Balance of Principal of		$ 824,161.29

Consisting of:

Cash in Bank	$ 10,447.99	
Mortgages	453,910.55	
Corporate Stocks	141,393.90	
Rental Building (Net)	112,800.00	
Municipal Bonds (Part)	105,608.85	
	$ 824,161.29	

Second as to Income:

The Executor Charges Himself With:

Business Income	$ 32,000.00	
Interest on Mortgages	106,208.87	
Dividends Received	16,720.28	
Interest on Municipal Bonds	8,584.68	
Rental Income	27,500.00	
Interest on Government Bonds	5,500.00	$ 196,513.83

The Executor Credits Himself With:

Office Expenses	$ 18,700.00
Building Repairs	2,980.00
Insurance	1,540.00
Utilities	4,700.00
Real Estate Taxes	1,950.00

(continued)

Depreciation	7,200.00	
Interest Expense	237.50	
Income Taxes Paid	55,674.00	
Distributions of Income	36,000.00	128,981.50
Leaving a Balance of Income of		$ 67,532.33

Consisting of:		
Cash in Bank	$	4,732.33
Government Bonds		50,000.00
Municipal Bonds (Part)		12,800.00
	$	67,532.33

FIGURE 5-10 continued

This final settlement statement was approved by the court and the executor was directed to turn the remaining assets over to the beneficiaries, in this case the widow only. Figure 5-11 shows the entry for this distribution.

FIGURE 5-11

407	Distributions of Principal	824,161.29	
600	Distributions of Income	67,532.33	
113	Allowance for Depreciation	7,200.00	
101	Principal Cash		10,447.99
102	Income Cash		4,732.33
105	Mortgages Receivable		453,910.55
107	Corporate Stocks		141,393.90
108	Municipal Bonds		118,408.85
111	Rental Building		120,000.00
119	Government Bonds		50,000.00

Distribution was now complete, the administration of the estate was finished, and only one more entry was needed to close the books completely. The accountant made this entry, as seen in Figure 5-12.

FIGURE 5-12

300	Estate Principal	1,397,751.68	
301	Assets Not Inventoried	10,000.00	
500	Estate Income	103,532.33	
401	Debts of Decedent		7,572.00
402	Funeral Expenses		2,900.00
403	Administration Expenses		75,880.00
404	Estate and Inheritance Taxes		256,683.00
405	Gains and Losses on Realization		5,605.39
406	Legacies Paid		11,000.00
407	Distributions of Principal		1,048,111.29
600	Distributions of Income		103,532.33

This entry resulted in the complete closing of every account in the estate's ledger.

CHAPTER SIX

Accounting for a Trust

6

Accounting for a trust is usually somewhat easier than for an estate. There are no debts of a decedent, no funeral expenses, no legacies or (most often) partial distributions, and there is no difficulty in discovering or evaluating the entity's assets.

The origin of a trust is usually well planned and the directives governing its administration and accounting are usually more explicit, so a trust might be thought of as a more self-contained entity than most estates are.

But again, the principles and rules of fiduciary accounting apply equally to both estates and trusts; the few points of difference are given in this chapter.

Theory of Trust Accounting

As with any fiduciary, the most important requirement for accounting for any trust is the proper segregation of principal and income.

Perhaps the greatest difference in trusts and estates, in general, is due to the fact that a decedent's will seldom contains anything very specific governing the determination of principal or income, anything that will override the established legal requirements regarding the segregation between the two, but a trust instrument very often goes into quite a bit of detail in defining exactly what shall be considered income, what shall be considered principal, and so on, and these directions govern completely—they take precedence over any contrary provisions of state law.

In cases where the trust instrument is not very explicit, the laws of the various states give the trustee some guidelines to follow, and most states have even adopted the Uniform Principal and Income Act or the Revised Uniform Principal and Income Act, spelling out the differences between principal and income in some detail. Where the law is silent or obscure on a question of allocation, or if the trust instrument leaves such questions to the discretion of the trustee, the trustee must make his choice in a prudent manner consistent with his basic obligation of impartiality among the different beneficiaries.

A trust's principal is not fixed or determined "as of" a certain date with its income taking place "after" that date, as it is with an estate. Instead, transactions taking place long after the establishment of the trust can affect its principal—things generally considered to be income are not always income but are principal.

As examples, depreciation—usually considered an income-deduction item— might be chargeable to the trust's principal; gains and losses on sales might also be items affecting principal rather than income; there might even be some operating-type expenses which the trust grantor has directed shall be charged to principal; it is even possible for a trust grantor to direct that dividend income, for example, shall be a credit to principal rather than to income!

Such determinations simply depend on the wishes of the trust grantor, as expressed by him in the trust instrument. His wishes, no matter how unusual or odd or even foolish, will govern. His main concern, in many cases, is for a certain amount of income to be produced for some beneficiary, so he will spell out just what he wants to have considered as income.

A trustee must shape his operations to any directions given in the trust instrument, and his accountant must also be completely familiar with these directions (and with state law) in order to see that the fiduciary accounting income produced by the accounting system is exactly in accordance with the grantor's wishes, even though that income might be very different from ordinary accounting income or taxable income.

The Opening Entry

The opening entry for a trust was described earlier—simply debit an asset account for each asset (or kind of asset) given to the trustee and credit Trust Principal for the total. Fair market values at the date of the transfer will be used.

If there is a mortgage against any of the property, it should be recorded in the opening entry—not always done with an estate. Assumption of any other liabilities by the trustee would be extremely rare.

Chart of Accounts

The illustrative chart of accounts for an estate, given in Figure 2-1, could be used equally well for a trust, with a few changes in account titles. A trust's chart of accounts might be as shown in Figure 6-1.

FIGURE 6-1

Illustrative Chart of Accounts
for a Trust

Assets:

100 - Petty Cash
101 - Principal Cash
102 - Income Cash
103 - Notes Receivable
104 - Bonds
105 - Interest Receivable
106 - Stocks
107 - Real Estate
108 - Allowance for Depreciation
109 - Miscellaneous Assets
110 -
111 -
112 -

Liabilities:

200 - Notes Payable
201 - Mortgage Payable
202 - Payroll Taxes Deducted
203 -
204 -

Net Worth (Principal):

300 - Trust Principal
301 - Additional Principal
400 - Gains Applicable to Principal
401 - Losses Applicable to Principal
402 - Administrative Expenses, Principal
403 - Dividends Applicable to Principal
404 - Distributions of Principal
405 -
406 -

Net Worth (Income):

500 - Trust Income
600 - Distributions of Income

Income:

700 - Interest Income
701 - Dividends Received
702 - Rental Income
703 - Partnership Income
704 - Gains Applicable to Income
705 -
706 -
707 -
708 -

Expenses:

800 - Salaries
801 - Office Rent
802 - Office Expenses
803 - Telephone
804 - Repairs
805 - Insurance
806 - Utilities
807 - Real Estate Taxes
808 - Payroll Taxes
809 - Interest Expenses
810 - Travel Expenses
811 - Commissions on Collections
812 - Depreciation Expense
813 - Miscellaneous Expense
814 - Income Taxes Paid
815 - Losses Applicable to Income
816 - Administrative Expenses, Income
817 -
818 -
819 -
820 -

Administrative Expenses

Determination of the proper "fiduciary accounting income" for *that particular fiduciary* is the trust accountant's major responsibility, and he will find that it is likely that the treatment of administrative expenses will have a greater effect on this than the treatment of any other item will have.

An estate's administrative expenses are proper charges against principal, but this is not always true with those of a trust. The trust instrument should say whether these expenses (trustee's fee, attorney and accountant fees, recording fees, and others) should be charged to the trust's principal or to its income, or in part to each, and this will govern. If it does not, state law will, with many laws saying that one-half shall be charged to income, the remainder to principal; the accounting for these expenses must be in accordance with any such directive. Obviously, this will have a very pronounced effect on the trust's income.

Again, ordinary accounting principles as well as tax accounting considerations must be ignored in determining the correct income for any particular trust; the trust instrument, and perhaps state law, will control.

Capital Gains and Losses

Another transaction that might have an unusual effect on a trust's income is a capital gain or loss.

If a trustee has the power to sell some of the trust's property, he might do so at a price either greater or less than the value he was charged with as a part of the trust's principal. Is this gain or loss applicable to the trust's income or does it change the amount of the trust's principal? The trust instrument will govern; it might provide for either treatment. But if the instrument fails to answer this question, state law will give the answer.

Still, if such a transaction is applicable to principal rather than to income this does not mean that it can be ignored for income tax purposes. It is still a capital gain or loss on the fiduciary income tax return.

Depreciation Treatment

Another item that might or might not affect the fiduciary accounting income is depreciation.

If there is depreciable (or depletable) property in the trust, should depreciation expense be charged and the decrease in value of the property be funded through a depreciation allowance as in ordinary accounting? This again depends on just what the trust instrument might have to say about it. If it mentions or provides for depreciation, this indicates that the trust grantor was aware of this and that he intended for the trust income to bear the expense of depreciation;

the accounting system, then, must provide for it and fiduciary accounting income will be income after depreciation.

If the trust instrument is silent regarding depreciation, state law will govern. Most often, the laws provide for depreciation to be considered and charged against income, but otherwise depreciation must be ignored in the accounting system, and in this case the fiduciary accounting income will not be reduced by any depreciation.

But even if depreciation is not provided for in the trust's books, this does not mean that it cannot be used as a deduction for income tax purposes. Fiduciary accounting income will be adjusted for any allowable depreciation in arriving at taxable income.

Other Expense and Income Items

The allocation of expenses other than the ones mentioned above is usually in accordance with general accounting principles, but, as always, the grantor might have included some contrary provisions in the trust instrument. And the same thing is true in connection with the various items of income a trust might have.

Expense Items

For the most part the expenses applicable to income include the ordinary expenses incurred in the administration, management, and preservation of the trust property, taxes on the property, insurance, interest, ordinary repairs, and so on; court costs, attorney fees, and other fees in proceedings if the matter primarily concerns the income interest; and income taxes levied on the trust's income.

Charges against principal include all administrative expenses not charged to income, special compensation of a trustee, expenses incurred directly in connection with principal, court costs and fees primarily concerning matters of principal, and others. Also, principal charges include the costs of investing and reinvesting principal, payments on the principal of an indebtedness, and expenses in maintaining or defending any action to construe the trust or protect it or the property or to assure the title of the property. And, of course, extraordinary repairs or capital improvements to the trust property, including special assessments, are proper charges to principal.

Income Items

As for a trust's receipts, these usually cause little difficulty and are allocated as they would be in ordinary accounting practice. Common items applicable to income would include rents from real and personal property, interest on loans or notes or mortgages, interest on bank accounts or corporate or government bonds, ordinary corporate dividends, income from a business or farming operation, income from a partnership or other fiduciary, and any other return in money or property derived from the use of the trust principal. Occasionally an apportionment of income is necessary, as when a receipt includes income accruing up to the date of creation of a trust (principal) and that accruing afterward (income).

Receipts applicable to principal would include, among others, simple repayment of loans, sale of an asset of the principal, and any other profit or loss resulting upon any change in form of the principal.

Other Transactions

There are a few other transactions, not too frequently encountered, which the trust's accountant should be aware of because of their possible effect on the trust's income. These are seldom thought of by a grantor in creating a trust, but if they are, his directions will, of course, govern; otherwise, state law will have to be consulted.

One such transaction is a corporate distribution of its own shares, such as a stock dividend or a stock split. This would, in practically all states, apply to principal. The same is true with stock rights and with liquidating dividends. Dividends made by a regulated investment company from its ordinary income apply to trust income, but those from capital gains, depletion, and the like are principal.

The amortization of premium or discount on bonds is usually ignored, and the proceeds from their sale or redemption is generally an increase or decrease in principal.

The proceeds from property taken on eminent domain proceedings and proceeds of insurance on losses of property constituting a part of principal will apply to the trust's principal.

There might be a number of other unusual but troublesome transactions demanding a decision as to their proper treatment. Again, a directive might be found in the statutes but, if not, the decision of the trustee, acting in good faith, will be upheld.

The Payment of Income Taxes

The income taxes paid by a trust on its net taxable income are considered as an operating expense rather than a charge against principal. When paid, they are debited to an expense account. Of course, the trust instrument could provide otherwise, but it is more logical for income to bear the expense.

It might be argued that any portion of the income taxes attributable to income that was added to Trust Principal, such as capital gains, should be charged against principal rather than income, but, for practical purposes, this is very seldom considered.

Distributions to Beneficiaries

Income distributions to beneficiaries will cause no accounting difficulties. They are simply charged to the Distributions of Income account, but if there is more than one beneficiary it would be good to make notations in the ledger account of the names and amounts each time.

If distributions of principal are authorized, such distributions are debited to the Distributions of Principal account, and the total value of the principal is reduced accordingly.

The two distributions accounts will remain open on the books until the final termination of the trust, but their balances can be combined with their related Trust Principal and Trust Income accounts at any time to determine the current status and amount of the undistributed principal and income of the trust.

Charitable Distributions

It is not at all uncommon for a trust instrument to provide for distributions to charitable organizations; in fact, some trusts even provide for no distributions except charitable ones.

A trust's contribution to a charity is never treated as an expense. It would not be proper for a trustee to charge income with such a payment, which is certainly not a proper operating expense. Charitable contributions are, instead, distributions, and they are made only as provided for in the trust instrument.

A trust instrument might provide for a charitable distribution to be made from income or from principal or both. The provision will, of course, govern the accountant in recording the distribution—it will simply be charged to the proper distribution account, the same as with a distribution to an individual beneficiary.

But as with several other disbursements, charitable distributions will be treated as expenses for income tax purposes even though charged to the Trust Principal rather than the Trust Income account, and will be one of the items used in adjusting fiduciary accounting income to taxable income.

Summary

The special features of accounting for a trust are as follows:

1. A trust instrument is more likely to contain specific directions regarding the treatment of various items as principal or as income than a decedent's will is.

2. Practically the same chart of accounts may be used for a trust as for an estate, with only a few changes in account titles.

3. The trust accountant must first pay very careful attention to any directions in the trust instrument governing principal and income allocations or, in the absence of certain directions, to state law.

CHAPTER **Seven**

Case Study in Trust Accounting

7

To illustrate the application of the principles and procedures used in accounting for a trust, a case study is given here. The size, makeup, objectives, and transactions in this case are rather typical, and the facts of the case are as follows.

Sarah Gray, a widow, created an irrevocable, inter-vivos trust on January 1, 1982, and named William Marshall as the Trustee of this trust.

Mrs. Gray established the trust in order to divert a portion of her large annual taxable income to lower bracket taxpayers (her two children and the trust itself), to help her favorite charity for many years, possibly even after her own death, and to provide income for her children while withholding any large amount of property from them until they would be old enough to handle it more wisely.

The trust was established to last for a period of ten years, after which time one-half of the trust principal and one-half of any undistributed income shall be turned over to Mrs. Gray's son, John Gray, who is now 22, and the other one-half to her daughter, Mary, now 19.

The trust instrument provides that, each year, ten percent of the trust income shall be distributed to the United Givers Fund and that one-half of the remainder of the trust income shall be distributed to the son, John Gray. The trustee is given discretionary power to either accumulate the balance of the income or to distribute any portion of the remainder that he sees fit to the daughter, Mary Gray.

The trust instrument further provides that there is to be no provision for depreciation and that all capital gains and losses shall be attributable to corpus rather than to income. It provides that seventy percent of all administrative expenses shall be charged to principal and thirty percent to income.

The trustee is required to make an annual accounting, at the end of each calendar year, to the beneficiaries and to the grantor, even though no such accounting is required by any court.

The Trust Inventory

The following assets were turned over to the trustee on January 1, 1982, and they are shown at their fair market values on that date:

Cash	$ 50,000.00
Corporate Bonds	300,000.00
Municipal Bonds	100,000.00
Ten Rental Houses	250,000.00
	$700,000.00

The Bookkeeping System

The first step in establishing a set of books for this trust was the plotting of a chart of accounts for the general ledger. The trust's accountant decided on the chart shown in Figure 7-1, based on the kind of assets being transferred to the trust and his expectations of the nature of the transactions likely to occur during the life of the trust.

FIGURE 7-1

CHART OF ACCOUNTS

Assets:

  101 - Principal Cash
  102 - Income Cash
  103 - Corporate Bonds
  104 - Municipal Bonds
  105 - Rental Houses
  106 -
  107 -

Liabilities:

  201 -
  202 -

Net Worth - Principal:

  300 - Trust Principal
  301 - Additions to Principal
  400 - Gains Applicable to Principal
  401 - Losses Applicable to Principal
  402 - Administrative Expenses, Principal
  403 - Distributions of Principal

Net Worth - Income:

  500 - Trust Income
  600 - Distributions of Income

Income:

  700 - Tax Exempt Interest
  701 - Taxable Interest
  702 - Rental Income
  703 - Other Income
  704 -
  705 -
  706 -

Expenses:

  800 - Administrative Expenses, Income
  801 - Rental Expenses
  802 - Income Taxes Paid
  803 -
  804 -
  805 -
  806 -

It was very possible, of course, that other accounts might need to be added later as the administration of the trust progressed, but this would cause no trouble.

Other Books Used

A general journal was provided, as usual, for recording the opening entry, adjusting and closing entries, and any other entries that would not lend themselves easily to columnar journals.

A subsidiary ledger was established for the rental houses, as there were ten of these in the trust. Another subsidiary ledger was needed for the corporate bonds, and a third subsidiary ledger was provided for the municipal bonds. Since numerous individual items were included in these three catagories of assets, and since it was possible that there might be transactions involving various individual items, a detailed record of each was considered most desirable.

It did not appear that a very large number of daily transactions would occur, so a combination cash receipts-disbursements journal was thought to be satisfactory. This journal contained the following column headings:

> Date
> Payee or Explanation
> Check or Receipt Number
>
> Dr. Principal Cash, No. 101
> Cr. Principal Cash, No. 101
> Dr. Income Cash, No. 102
> Cr. Income Cash, No. 102
>
> Cr. Tax Exempt Interest, No. 700
> Cr. Taxable Interest, No. 701
> Cr. Rental Income, No. 702
>
> Dr. Administrative Expenses, Principal, No. 402
> Dr. Administrative Expenses, Income, No. 800
> Dr. Rental Expenses, No. 801
> Dr. Distributions of Principal, No. 403
> Dr. Distributions of Income, No. 600
>
> Other Accounts - Account Number
> Other Accounts - Debit
> Other Accounts - Credit

As a reminder, in preparing the headings for this journal a pair of columns for Principal Cash and a pair for Income Cash should be provided.

The Opening Entry

The entry to open the books for this trust was made in the general journal, as follows:

101	Principal Cash	50,000.00	
103	Corporate Bonds	300,000.00	
104	Municipal Bonds	100,000.00	
105	Rental Houses	250,000.00	
300	Trust Principal		700,000.00

Remember—the assets should be recorded at their fair market values at the date of the transfer to the trust; this is because these are the values with which the trustee is charged, they are the values which the grantor had in mind when creating the trust, and they are the values on which the trustee is expected to produce income. These values certainly might not be correct for income tax purposes, but they are proper for fiduciary accounting purposes. A subsidiary record of the bases for income tax purposes should be maintained.

Transactions for the Year 1982

The trustee's transactions for the year 1982 are given below. Most of the entries for these were made in the cash journal, but they are given here in general journal form, along with the ledger account numbers to which they would be posted.

1. Early in January 1982 the trustee purchased some corporate stocks for $35,000.00

106	Corporate Stocks	35,000.00	
101	Principal Cash		35,000.00

   One of the principal duties of a trustee is to try to produce a satisfactory income on the assets. Since a large amount of nonproductive cash was turned over to the trustee it would have been foolish not to invest it rather quickly, so stocks were purchased. This necessitated a new account, not originally provided, Account No. 106, Corporate Stocks.

2. The trustee sold the above stocks late in the year for $38,000.00.

101	Principal Cash	38,000.00	
106	Corporate Stocks		35,000.00
400	Gains Applicable to Principal		3,000.00

   According to the trust instrument, this gain must go to principal rather than to income. It will be taxable gain for income tax purposes but it has no effect whatever on Fiduciary Accounting Income, which is always the income determined in accordance with the terms of the trust instrument.

3. Interest collected on the corporate bonds during the year amounted to $24,000.00.

102	Income Cash	24,000.00	
701	Taxable Interest		24,000.00

   This is a typical item which does, certainly, apply to the income of the trust.

4. Interest income from the municipal bonds was $5,500.00 for the year.

102	Income Cash	5,500.00	
700	Tax Exempt Interest		5,500.00

   For fiduciary accounting purposes, this interest might just as well have been credited to an account simply called "Interest Income," as the source of the interest is unimportant. But for convenience in preparing the income tax return later, it is better to keep the non-taxable interest separate.

5. Rental income from the houses for the year amounted to $32,500.00.

102	Income Cash	32,500.00	
702	Rental Income		32,500.00

This is another typical item of income for a fiduciary.

6. The trustee sold one of the rental houses, listed on the books at $26,000.00, for $25,000.00.

101	Principal Cash	25,000.00	
401	Losses Applicable to Principal	1,000.00	
105	Rental Houses		26,000.00

This loss is also applicable to Principal as directed by the terms of the trust instrument. It has no effect on the fiduciary accounting income though it will certainly be considered later in preparing the fiduciary income tax return. Again, Fiduciary Accounting Income is the income contemplated by the trust instrument, and tax considerations must be ignored in strict fiduciary accounting.

7. Rental Expenses for insurance, taxes, repairs, collection fees, and others amounted to $7,500.00 for the year.

801	Rental Expenses	7,500.00	
102	Income Cash		7,500.00

Separate accounts could be used, of course, for the various rental expenses rather than have them lumped in one account; this is optional with the accountant, who will be governed by the probable need for more detailed information later—such as in preparing tax returns.

8. Dividends received on the corporate stocks owned were $1,050.00.

102	Income Cash	1,050.00	
704	Dividends Received		1,050.00

Another new account must be added in the general ledger—Account Number 704, Dividends Received.

9. The trustee bought a one-year certificate of deposit in a savings and loan association for $40,000.00.

107	Certificate of Deposit	40,000.00	
101	Principal Cash		40,000.00

Again, as cash accumulates through collections and sales, the trustee should try to keep it invested and working. A new account is needed for the certificate of deposit.

10. Interest received on the certificate of deposit was $1,600.00.

102	Income Cash	1,600.00	
701	Taxable Interest		1,600.00

Notice that although the certificate was purchased with principal cash, the income from it goes to income cash.

11. The trustee invested another $30,000.00 in corporate bonds.

103	Corporate Bonds	30,000.00	
101	Principal Cash		30,000.00

12. The trustee's fee for the year, plus other incidental administrative expenses, amounted to $4,000.00.

402	Administrative Expenses, Prin.	2,800.00	
800	Administrative Expenses, Income	1,200.00	
101	Principal Cash		2,800.00
102	Income Cash		1,200.00

The allocation of these expenses between principal and income is in accordance with the directions in the trust instrument. But the portion charged to principal will still be deductible for income tax purposes, so this is one of the possibly several adjustments which will have to be made later to bring Fiduciary Accounting Income to Taxable Income.

13. Depreciation on the rental houses was computed to be $6,840.00 for the year 1982. No entry is made for this because the trust instrument directs that depreciation shall be ignored; fiduciary accounting income is, therefore, not affected by depreciation. But it is still allowable for income tax purposes, so this is another of the adjustments needed later in computing taxable income.

14. At the end of the year 1982 the trust's income (fiduciary accounting income) was computed to be $55,950.00. The trustee distributed ten percent of this, or $5,595.00, to the United Givers Fund and one-half of the remainder, or $25,177.50, to Mrs. Gray's son.

600	Distributions of Income	30,772.50	
102	Income Cash		30,772.50

The correct fiduciary accounting income was $55,950.00, ignoring depreciation, capital gains and losses, and a portion of the administrative expenses—just as the grantor directed in the trust instrument. This was, therefore, the figure on which the distributions had to be based. Note that the payment to the charity was not an expense. It was a distribution of income just like the distribution to the son. However, it is an expense for income tax purposes and will be considered later in preparing the fiduciary income tax return.

15. The trustee decided to make a discretionary distribution to Mrs. Gray's daughter in the amount of $18,000.00.

600	Distributions of Income	18,000.00	
102	Income Cash		18,000.00

The trust instrument gave the trustee the power to make such a distribution, in any amount, or to withhold it each year.

It was not possible for the trust accountant to compute the amount of the fiduciary income tax which would be payable for the year 1982 in time to write a check for it by the end of the year, but no entry was necessary for this. Fiduciary accounting is on the cash basis and the payment of income taxes will simply be recorded when the check is written and the tax return for the fiduciary filed early in 1983.

Closing for the Year 1982

A trial balance of the trust ledger at December 31, 1982, is seen in Figure 7-2.

FIGURE 7-2

Trial Balance—December 31, 1982

		Debit	Credit
101	Principal Cash	5,200.00	
102	Income Cash	7,177.50	
103	Corporate Bonds	330,000.00	
104	Municipal Bonds	100,000.00	
105	Rental Houses	224,000.00	
107	Certificate of Deposit	40,000.00	
300	Trust Principal		700,000.00
400	Gains Applicable to Principal		3,000.00
401	Losses Applicable to Principal	1,000.00	
402	Administrative Expenses, Principal	2,800.00	
500	Trust Income		—
600	Distributions of Income	48,772.50	
700	Tax Exempt Interest		5,500.00
701	Taxable Interest		25,600.00
702	Rental Income		32,500.00
704	Dividends Received		1,050.00
800	Administrative Expenses, Income	1,200.00	
801	Rental Expenses	7,500.00	
		767,650.00	767,650.00

No adjusting entries were necessary, as no accruals of income or of expenses need be made when the books are on the cash basis. The only entry needed is the usual annual entry closing all of the income and expense accounts into Trust Income, as follows:

700	Tax Exempt Interest	5,500.00	
701	Taxable Interest	25,600.00	
702	Rental Income	32,500.00	
704	Dividends Received	1,050.00	
800	Administrative Expenses, Income		1,200.00
801	Rental Expenses		7,500.00
500	Trust Income		55,950.00

The Interim Report

After closing the books for the year, the trust's accountant prepared the annual report required by the trust instrument.

This report (Figure 7-3) was prepared in the charge and discharge statement form which was described earlier.

FIGURE 7-3

Sarah Gray Trust
William Marshall, Trustee

CHARGE AND DISCHARGE STATEMENT

For the Year Ended December 31, 1982

First as to Principal:

The Trustee Charges Himself with:

Assets Placed in Trust	$ 700,000.00	
Gains Applicable to Principal	3,000.00	$ 703,000.00

The Trustee Credits Himself with:

Losses Applicable to Principal	$ 1,000.00	
Administrative Expenses, Principal	2,800.00	3,800.00
Leaving a Balance of Principal of		$ 699,200.00

Consisting of:

Cash in Bank	$ 5,200.00	
Corporate Bonds	330,000.00	
Municipal Bonds	100,000.00	
Rental Houses	224,000.00	
Certificate of Deposit	40,000.00	
	$ 699,200.00	

Second as to Income:

The Trustee Charges Himself with:

Tax Exempt Interest	$ 5,500.00	
Taxable Interest	25,600.00	
Rental Income	32,500.00	
Dividends Received	1,050.00	$ 64,650.00

The Trustee Credits Himself with:

Administrative Expenses, Income	$ 1,200.00	
Rental Expenses	7,500.00	
Distributions of Income	48,772.50	57,472.50
Leaving a Balance of Income of		$ 7,177.50

Consisting of:
Cash in Bank

$ 7,177.50

The Remaining Trust Years

In this case the grantor, Sarah Gray, lived beyond the ten-year term of the trust, but assuming that she had died at the end of the fourth year, what changes would have had to be made to the trust accounting records?

No changes at all would have been necessary. A trust is a completely separate entity, apart from its grantor. Once established, the trust operates strictly on its own with no further directions from—or even need for—the grantor!

However, if one of the individual beneficiaries—the son, for example—died, the trust provisions applicable to him would lapse and cease to be effective. The trust instrument should provide for such an eventuality; it should state what should happen to the son's portion of the trust income in case of his death, and especially, what should become of the son's share of the principal and the undistributed income in that event.

The Years 1983 Through 1991

The remaining nine years of the trust term passed, with the transactions being much like those shown for the first year, and a trial balance of the ledger on December 31, 1991 (after the year-end entry closing income and expenses into Trust Income) was as shown in Figure 7-4.

FIGURE 7-4

Trial Balance—December 31, 1991

		Debit	Credit
101	Principal Cash	11,200.00	
102	Income Cash	17,288.50	
103	Corporate Bonds	330,000.00	
104	Municipal Bonds	105,000.00	
105	Rental Houses	174,000.00	
106	Corporate Stocks	20,000.00	
107	Certificates of Deposit	60,000.00	
300	Trust Principal		700,000.00
400	Gains Applicable to Principal		12,000.00
401	Losses Applicable to Principal	1,000.00	
402	Administrative Expenses, Principal	30,800.00	
500	Trust Income		482,862.00
600	Distributions of Income	445,573.50	
		1,194,862.00	1,194,862.00

The income and expense accounts had been closed each year, of course, but cumulative totals for each of these had been carried in the charge and discharge statement prepared each year, and the totals for the ten years were as follows:

700	Tax Exempt Income		55,500.00
701	Taxable Income		205,600.00
702	Rental Income		322,500.00
704	Dividends Received		1,050.00
800	Administrative Expense, Income	13,200.00	
801	Rental Expenses	70,500.00	
802	Income Taxes Paid	18,088.00	

The Final Report

The final report—cumulative for the entire ten-year period—was prepared prior to the distribution of the assets to the beneficiaries.

This report, in the usual charge and discharge statement form, is given in Figure 7-5.

FIGURE 7-5

Sarah Gray Trust
William Marshall, Trustee

CHARGE AND DISCHARGE STATEMENT

For the Period January 1, 1982, to December 31, 1991

First as to Principal:

The Trustee Charges Himself with:

Assets Placed in Trust	$ 700,000.00	
Gains Applicable to Principal	12,000.00	$ 712,000.00

The Trustee Credits Himself with:

Losses Applicable to Principal	$ 1,000.00	
Administrative Expenses, Principal	30,800.00	31,800.00
Leaving a Balance of Principal of		$ 680,200.00

Consisting of:

Cash in Bank	$ 11,200.00
Corporate Bonds	330,000.00
Municipal Bonds	105,000.00
Rental Houses	174,000.00
Certificates of Deposit (Portion)	40,000.00
Corporate Stocks	20,000.00
	$ 680,200.00

Second as to Income:

The Trustee Charges Himself with:

Tax Exempt Interest	$ 55,500.00	
Taxable Interest	205,600.00	
Rental Income	322,500.00	
Dividends Received	1,050.00	$ 584,650.00

The Trustee Credits Himself with:

Administrative Expenses, Income	$ 13,200.00	
Rental Expenses	70,500.00	
Income Taxes Paid	18,088.00	
Distributions of Income	445,573.50	547,361.50
Leaving a Balance of Income of		$ 37,288.50

Consisting of:

Cash in Bank	$ 17,288.50
Certificates of Deposit (Portion)	20,000.00
	$ 37,288.50

The Final Closing

The trustee made a final distribution of the principal and the income, one-half to the son and one-half to the daughter, in accordance with the terms of the trust instrument. The accountant's entry to record this distribution was as follows:

403	Distributions of Principal	680,200.00	
600	Distributions of Income	37,288.50	
101	Principal Cash		11,200.00
102	Income Cash		17,288.50
103	Corporate Bonds		330,000.00
104	Municipal Bonds		105,000.00
105	Rental Houses		174,000.00
106	Corporate Stocks		20,000.00
107	Certificates of Deposit		60,000.00

This entry closed out all of the asset accounts and left only the net worth accounts open. The final entry to close the trust books, which resulted in the closing of every account in the ledger was as follows:

300	Trust Principal	700,000.00	
400	Gains Applicable to Principal	12,000.00	
500	Trust Income	482,862.00	
401	Losses Applicable to Principal		1,000.00
402	Administrative Expenses, Principal		30,800.00
403	Distributions of Principal		680,200.00
600	Distributions of Income		482,862.00

Accounting for Other Fiduciaries

8

The term "fiduciary" is normally thought of in connection with either a trust or an estate; however, there are a number of other fiduciary capacities in which an individual or a bank trust department may be called upon to serve. These other fiduciary capacities are equally as important as serving as a fiduciary for an estate or trust, and the accounting requirements are very much the same as those for the estate or trust.

The committee, guardian, agent, and trustee in bankruptcy are other fiduciary capacities that are fairly common. The general rules of fiduciary accounting apply to the fiduciary serving in these capacities, except that the distinction between principal and income—so important in estates and trusts—is not necessary because there will be only one beneficiary for both the principal and the income.

However, each capacity has a few other points of difference that are given in this chapter.

Committees as Fiduciaries

A committee is an individual or the trust department of a bank that is appointed by a court to manage the financial affairs of an adult individual who has become mentally incapacitated and is therefore unable to manage his or her own financial affairs. The appointment of a committee is not a simple court procedure, since it requires that the individual be declared mentally incompetent. In some states, the procedure requires a jury trial and is very expensive as a result of the court costs and legal fees involved. The committee functions under the authority provided in the statutes of the state in which the appointment is made.

Good financial planning can provide means by which the procedure of having a committee appointed can be avoided in the event of mental incompetency. One method is to have an inter-vivos trust that can receive the individual's property in the event of incompetency; a limited power of attorney is required to authorize someone to transfer the property to the trust on behalf of the person who has become incompetent. Another way to avoid court proceedings is, during the course of planning, to give an individual or a bank trust department a general power of attorney which specifies that it will not be terminated by the mental incompetency of the individual granting the power.

It is also possible for a person to grant a power of attorney that will not become effective unless the individual becomes incompetent. If that does happen, the person named in the power of attorney, who is known as an attorney-in-fact, can legally manage the incompetent's financial affairs completely outside of the jurisdiction of the court.

The Committee's Accounting System

The accounting system needed for a committee is much the same as that needed for a trust. The specific accounts that will be used in the chart of accounts will depend on the type of assets coming into the hands of the committee for management. If the incompetent is the owner of a business that is operated as a sole proprietorship, the committee may be required to run the business if the court so directs. In that case, a separate set of records should be maintained for the business and a single account in the books of the committee should reflect the investment in the business.

There is no need to separate income cash and principal cash on the books for a committee or to have two different equity accounts, as the incompetent individual has the beneficial ownership of and the right to the income as well as to the principal. In most cases, the income will be used to pay for the physical needs of the incompetent, and if the income is not sufficient, the committee may use principal to fulfill those needs. Depending on the physical condition of the incompetent and the degree of incompetency, the incompetent may be confined to a nursing home or a hospital, in which case the physical needs can be very expensive.

The bookkeeping system for the committee should be set up in such a manner that the filing of income tax returns for the incompetent will be expedited; it is the committee's responsibility to see that income tax returns are prepared and filed for the incompetent. It is not necessary that the committee file a fiduciary income tax return. The federal Form 1040 and the state form required are all that need to be filed. The committee should use the incompetent's social security number rather than a federal identification number in all cases where such a number is required.

After the chart of accounts has been decided upon and the necessary journals and ledgers established, an opening entry should be made to record all of the property that has come into the hands of the committee. The property should be recorded at its value on the date it came into the hands of the committee, which is normally the date the committee is appointed by the court. The committee's responsibility for the property begins when the court appointment is effective, and the value as of that date is used in order to provide a means of judging the committee's performance with regard to the property. A subsidiary record of the tax bases of the property should be maintained.

The Accounting Period

The committee may be faced with a need for two accounting periods—one for the filing of the incompetent's income tax returns and one for the preparation of reports to the court—but this should be avoided if possible. If the committee is likely to be serving for a number of years, the court may be petitioned for permission to file an accounting for a first short period in order to make the due date for the report to the court coincide with the end of the incompetent's tax year.

When the end of the accounting period is reached, the closing procedure as demonstrated for estates and trusts in earlier chapters should be followed. But again, the distinction between the income equity and the principal equity does not need to be maintained in the closing procedure since the incompetent is the owner of both equities.

The Committee's Reports

Since the committee is appointed by the court, it remains under the jurisdiction of the court and periodical accountings to the court must be made.

There is no uniformity in the format in which the report must be presented; however, some courts may specify a required form for the report. Generally, the Charge and Discharge Statement illustrated in Figure 3-3 will be adequate to satisfy the requirements of the court. The frequency of the report will vary from state to state, but if the report is not required on an annual basis it is a good idea for the committee to prepare and submit a report annually if the court will permit. After the report is filed and accepted by the court, the committee is discharged from any potential personal liability arising from the transactions covered by the report.

In order for the committee to be released from the responsibility of his position, it must file a final settlement with the court and it must be accepted. Prior to the filing of the final settlement, the committee must properly dispose of the property for which he is responsible by turning it over to the proper person. If the committee is being replaced by a successor committee, the property must be turned over to the successor who will assume responsibility as of the date appointed by the court. In the event of the death of the incompetent, the property is turned over to the executor or administrator appointed by the court. And there have been cases where the incompetent has regained competency, and the committee returns the property to the individual.

A normal closing procedure should be followed as of the date on which the committee's responsibility ends. Subsequent to the normal closing, a final closing entry should be made in which all asset, liability, and equity accounts are closed.

The Guardian as Fiduciary

A guardian is an individual or the trust department of a bank that is appointed by a court to manage the financial affairs of a minor. The guardian may be appointed to manage property that a minor has inherited or received as a gift. In other cases, the guardian may receive distributions from a trust established for the benefit of the minor and use the distributions for the minor's living and educational expenses. The guardian functions under authority provided in the statutes of the state in which the appointment is made.

In many cases the guardian has the responsibility for the person of the minor as well as the minor's financial affairs, but in some cases the guardian is responsible only for the minor's financial affairs while someone else is responsible for the person of the minor. If the minor has a parent living, the parent is appointed as guardian unless there are reasons why another person should be appointed. If there are no surviving parents, the guardian to be appointed may be specified in the will of the deceased parents, but if no specification is made in the will, the court will decide who is to be appointed, taking into consideration all the facts of the specific case.

The guardian serves until the minor reaches his majority. The age of majority varies from state to state, but in most states the minor is considered to have reached his or her majority upon attaining the age of eighteen. When the minor reaches his majority, the guardian turns over to him the assets being managed and files a final accounting with the court. After the final accounting has been accepted by the court, the guardian is released from the responsibility of his position.

If the minor should die before reaching the age of majority, the guardian would transfer the minor's property to the executor or administrator appointed by the court and then file the final accounting with the court.

Accounting for a Guardianship

The accounting requirements for a guardian are very much the same as for a committee. Basically, the only difference between the committee and the guardian is the age of the individual they represent. The minor has ownership of and the right to the principal as well as the income from the property being held by the guardian; therefore, the distinction between principal and income does not have to be maintained in the accounting system.

The selection of accounts for the chart of accounts, journals to be used, and the closing procedures for the guardian require the same considerations as for the committee discussed in the preceding section. The preparation of periodical accountings to the court will also follow the same procedures as set forth for the committee.

After the final accounting has been filed, the accounting records of the guardian are closed by using the closing procedures previously discussed.

Agents as Fiduciaries

An agent is an individual or the trust department of a bank that acts for or in place of an individual or a legal entity, such as a corporation, by authority granted by the individual or the legal entity. The individual or entity granting the authority is known as the principal, and the relationship created between the principal and the agent is known as an agency.

The agent operates within the framework of the authority that is granted by the principal. The authority may be granted in an agency agreement entered into by the two parties or it may be granted in a power of attorney. Depending on the type of authority granted, it may be necessary to record the agency agreement or power of attorney with the clerk of the court having jurisdiction over such recordings so the agreement will be a matter of public record, and such a recording is necessary when the agent is going to complete real estate transactions for the principal. But even though the agency agreement may be recorded with the clerk of a court, the agent's transactions do not come under the jurisdiction of the court, and the agent does not have to file periodic accountings with the court.

The scope of authority granted to an agent by the principal may be so broad as to be all-encompassing or the authority granted may be so restricted as to provide authority with regard to a single transaction. If the authority is set forth in a *general* power of attorney, the agent will have the authority to enter into any transactions that the principal could transact on his or her own behalf. In some states the statutes provide that the authority granted in a power of attorney remains in effect if the principal should become mentally incapacitated. If the statutes do not have such a provision, it is customary to draft a provision in the power of attorney stating that the authority granted is to survive the mental incapacity of the principal. Some agency agreements and powers of attorney are drafted in such a manner that the authority granted shall not become effective *unless* the principal becomes mentally incapacitated. The authority granted to an agent does not survive the death of the principal.

The Agent's Accounting Records

The accounting records required by an agent will depend on the scope of the agent's authority and the type of transactions involved. In some cases, deposit slips and cancelled checks from a special bank account might suffice, while in other cases the accounting records might be very complex.

When considering the chart of accounts for an agent, the following questions should be answered:

1. Is the nature of the agency such that it will last for a long period of time or will its duration be short?
2. Is the principal turning assets over to the agent to be managed?
3. Will the agent be responsible for the operation of a going business?
4. Will the agent's records be used for the preparation of the principal's income tax returns?
5. Will the agent's records be used for the preparation of periodic accountings to a court that has jurisdiction over the principal in some capacity?
6. What type of transactions will the agent have with regard to the agency agreement?

Asset accounts should be included in the chart for the purpose of recording the assets placed in the hands of the agent. If a going business is to be operated along with other responsibilities under the agreement, a separate set of books should be maintained for the business, with the business books tied to the agent's books by an investment account.

> An agent may be responsible only for the collection of income and the remitting of the income to the principal. In that case, the agent's books might include only one asset account (cash in bank), the necessary income accounts, and an account in the equity section that is to be charged when income is remitted to the principal.

An opening entry should be made on the agent's books to record the assets being held by the agent for the principal. The valuations to be used will depend upon the degree of responsibility and authority the agent has over the property. If the agent has full investment authority over the assets, the assets should be recorded at their fair market value on the date they are transferred to the agent. If the agent does not have investment responsibility over the assets being held or is holding them in a custodial capacity, they could also be recorded at the fair market value on the date they are transferred to the agent, but it would probably be more convenient and better facilitate the submission of information for income tax return preparation to record the assets at the principal's income tax basis in the property.

> The distinction to be made in selecting the valuation to be used in the opening entry is that in cases where the agent has investment authority, it is important to record the assets at fair market value on the date they are transferred to the agent so there is a basis for the measurement of investment performance.

When an agent accepts the responsibility to collect income from investments that have not been transferred to him, it might be helpful to record the investments on his books at a nominal value of one dollar for control purposes. Such a recording is especially helpful if the investments over which the agent has collection responsibility are likely to change during the term of the agency.

Closing Procedures for the Agency

At the end of the accounting period for the agency, closing entries should be made in much the same manner as illustrated for a trust; however, as a general rule, the distinction between principal and income does not need to be made, since the principal to the agency agreement has the ownership of and right to both the principal and income held by the agent unless the agency agreement specifies otherwise.

The termination of an agency agreement may result from the terms of the agreement, a revocation of the agreement by the principal, or the death of the principal. In the event of the death of the principal, assets being held by the agent will be delivered to the executor or administrator appointed for the principal's estate. In the event of termination by the terms of the agreement or revocation by the principal, assets held by the agent will be disposed of in accordance with the terms of the agreement or as instructed by the principal.

After the agent has delivered the assets to the proper person, the normal closing procedure should be used with the books of the agent. Following the normal closing, a final entry should be made removing the asset and equity accounts from the books.

Fiduciaries for Bankrupts

The positions of receiver and of trustee in bankruptcy proceedings are fiduciary capacities that are extremely complex.

Bankruptcy proceedings are governed by the Federal Bankruptcy Act which is administered by the federal bankruptcy courts.

After a petition in bankruptcy is filed, the court may appoint a *receiver* to take charge of the property of the bankrupt party to protect the assets and the interests of the creditors. The receiver continues in his position until the creditors meet and appoint a *trustee* or until the petition is dismissed. The receiver and the trustee function under the jurisdiction of the bankruptcy court.

A trustee is either elected by the creditors or appointed by the court to act as the representative of the creditors and the agent of the court in administering the bankrupt estate. The trustee takes title to the bankrupt's assets, and it is the trustee's duty to collect this property.

After considering the exemption of some of the property held, as provided by the Bankruptcy Act, it is the trustee's responsibility to liquidate the assets by selling the bankrupt's property under the supervision of the court and to insure that his creditors are paid in the order of their priority.

The accounting records to be maintained by the receiver and the trustee must be designed in such a manner as to account for the bankrupt's assets, the transactions involved in the disposition of the assets, and the payment of claims to creditors. The accounting records must also be designed in such a manner as to facilitate the preparation of very detailed reports to the bankruptcy court and the creditors of the bankrupt.

The requirements of the accounting systems of receivers and trustees in bankruptcy are basically very much like those of other fiduciaries, but the Bankruptcy Act should be studied carefully for any special instructions that might affect the accounting—just as a will or trust instrument is studied to learn of unusual provisions affecting the estate or trust.

As for the reports of receivers and trustees, there is little similarity with those of other fiduciaries; specific kinds of report forms must be used for presentation to the bankruptcy court.

Summary

A summary of considerations for the preparation of accounting systems for other fiduciaries is as follows:

1. The distinction between principal and income is usually not important because the same person most often has the right to both.

2. The committee and guardian are court-appointed positions for the management of the financial affairs of individuals who are not capable of managing their own affairs, the committee being for an adult who is mentally incapacitated and the guardian being for a minor.

3. Periodic accountings to the court are required for both the committee and the guardian.

4. The agent acts for or in place of an individual or legal entity with authority set forth in an agency agreement or power of attorney, and the agent is not subject to the jurisdiction of the courts.

5. The accounts selected to be used in the chart of accounts will depend on the assets coming into the fiduciary's control and the type of transactions the fiduciary will be making.

6. In the accounting records for the agent, it will be necessary to distinguish between principal and income only if the agency agreement so requires.

7. In the opening entry for the committee and guardian, assets coming under the control of the fiduciary should be recorded at the fair market value on the date the court appointment is made.

8. In the opening entry for the agent, the valuation to be used in recording the assets depends on the degree of responsibility for the assets that the agent

has under the terms of the agency agreement. If the agent has full investment authority, the assets should be recorded at their fair market value on the date they are transferred to the agent. If full investment authority has not been granted to the agent, the principal's tax basis in the assets is probably the most convenient valuation to use.

9. Journals should be designed by giving consideration to both the types and volume of transactions that the fiduciary will encounter.

10. Annual closing entries are made at the end of the accounting periods.

11. The final closing takes place after the assets have been transferred to the proper person and the final accounting, if required, has been filed with the court.

CHAPTER Nine

Trust Company Fiduciary Accounting

9

The discussion of fiduciary accounting in previous chapters has been from the point of view of the use of a standard double-entry type of bookkeeping system. The accounting systems used by trust companies are based on a concept that is totally different from the standard double-entry system. Generally, when an accountant first encounters the type of system used by trust companies, there is concern in his mind as to how such a system can be used accurately.

On the surface, the records the accountant is given to work with look as though the checks and balances of the double-entry system are missing, but the accountant is looking at the records of only one account and not at the accounting system as a whole. The accounting system used by a trust company is designed to provide a means of accounting for a large number of trust accounts within a framework of controls over cash transactions and investments. When looking at one account, the accountant sees only one side of the accounting entry and, therefore, thinks he is dealing with a single-entry type of record.

Types of Systems Used by Trust Companies

Trust companies use basically one of two types of systems—a system manually posted with a posting machine or an electronic data processing system. The basic records produced by both systems are very similar. The format for the ledger card posted on the manual system and the format for the account ledger produced by a computer are the same.

The manual system has a subsidiary ledger for the assets in each fiduciary account, and it contains a ledger card for each asset held for the account. The electronic data processing system produces a list of assets held by each fiduciary account and shows the same information as the asset card in the manual system.

Preparation of reports and tax returns from the manual system requires a considerable amount of analyzing and summarizing. The electronic data processing system is capable of generating reports to beneficiaries and summaries for use in the preparation of tax returns.

Most trust companies now have the electronic data processing system; therefore, the remainder of this chapter will deal with that type of system only.

Basics of Trust Company Accounting

A trust company keeps its records for dozens—even hundreds—of fiduciary accounts in what is actually one set of books. Each individual fiduciary account is detailed in what might be thought of as a subsidiary ledger account within that one set of books.

The trust company maintains only *one* bank account for cash, one in which all principal cash and all income cash for *all* of its estates, trusts, guardianships, and other fiduciaries is deposited. And there might be only one account for all of the assets of *all* these fiduciaries. These two debit balance asset accounts are off-set by a credit balance account called "Trust Funds."

The general ledger—if it can be called that—is extremely simple. (Perhaps the term "general ledger" should not even be used, as there is really no such book; the control account balances are merely computer print-out totals.) Its chart of accounts consists basically of only

Cash in Bank (Dr.)
Trust Assets (Dr.)
Trust Funds (Cr.)

In actual practice, this chart would be expanded a bit. The accounts that might be used, along with a brief explanation of each, are as follows:

Trust Funds Uninvested—This is simply the account for cash in the bank, the one referred to above.

Trust Funds Invested—This account includes all securities, real estate, certificates of deposit, and all other assets owned except for cash in the bank.

Assets Maturing Receivable—This account, which is not used by all trust companies, is a temporary account for recording securities and other assets which are about to become due. When it is debited, "Trust Funds Invested" is credited. It simply serves as a reminder that a collection is to be made.

Interest Receivable—This account is used the same as the Asset Maturing Receivable account. As interest on investments is becoming due, this temporary account is used as a reminder and control.

Trust Funds—This credit balance account offsets the four accounts shown above. It is the trust company's responsibility account, its liability to the various beneficiaries of all the fiduciary accounts. In trust company parlance, the term "liability" is used to mean accountability to beneficiaries, not to mean "payables" as in ordinary accounting. There is no equity account, as such, used, but this Trust Funds account is the equivalent of an equity account.

So the trust company's general ledger will be very small. It is simply a group of control accounts, controlling the assets of *all* of the various fiduciary accounts the company handles and controlling the total of the trust company's obligation or accountability (or liability, as trust companies term it) to *all* of the various principal and income beneficiaries.

Each individual fiduciary account is, as mentioned before, just a subsidiary ledger account, and it shows that one fiduciary's net assets only. Therefore, any one fiduciary's ledger account would seem to be a single-entry account, but this is not really the case. It can be compared with the subsidiary ledger account for one account receivable in ordinary bookkeeping; this account, by itself, would seem to be single entry and incomplete, but of course it is a part of a double-entry system.

The average accountant, who is so double-entry, debit-credit-oriented, might have trouble believing in the efficiency of this kind of system, but it does work effectively, as proved by hundreds of trust companies over a long period of years.

The Account Ledger

The account ledger for one fiduciary account, illustrated in Figure 9-1, is the basic record of transactions generated by the system. It contains the date of each transaction, a detailed description of the transaction, and the amounts involved. There are three amount columns: principal cash, income cash, and assets. The two cash columns provide the ability to distinguish between the principal and the income of the fiduciary account. (Again, the trust company maintains only one actual bank account, the balance of which is equal to the total of all the principal and income cash balances maintained in the fiduciary accounts administered by the trust company.)

Figure 9-1

```
40-00305.00                                              ACCOUNT LEDGER
TR A U/A
SAMUEL DOUGLAS                                           PAGE 3
```

DATE		INCOME	PRINCIPAL	ASSETS
	BALANCE BROUGHT FORWARD 4/30/80	1029.66	1000.00−	22973.00
4/30	CK#14376 CNB INCOME FOR QTR ENDING 4-30-80 DEPOSIT TO CHECKING	1029.66−		
	BAL AS OF 4/30/80 21,973.00 **	.00 *	1000.00−*	22973.00 *
5/01	SALE OF TEMP FD		1000.00	1000.00−
	BAL AS OF 5/01/80 21,973.00 **	.00 *	.00 *	21973.00 *
5/06	CK#14438 CNB FEE FOR FISCAL YEAR ENDING 4-30-80	85.62−		
	BAL AS OF 5/06/80 21,887.38 **	85.62−*	.00 *	21973.00 *
5/08	SALE OF TEMP FUND		100.00	100.00−
	BAL AS OF 5/08/80 21,887.38 **	85.62−*	100.00 *	21873.00 *
5/12	INT TEMP FUND	24.65		
	BAL AS OF 5/12/80 21,912.03 **	60.97−*	100.00 *	21873.00 *
5/16	SALE OF TEMP FDS		1750.00	1750.00−
5/16	SALE OF IM FED FARM CR BKS 9.90% DUE 10-20-80 ACC INT 6.78 LOSS 7.10		999.68	1000.00−
5/16	CK#14556 INTERNAL REVENUE SERVICE US FIDUCIARY TAX RETURN 1041	2691.00−		
	BAL AS OF 5/16/80 19,220.71 **	2751.91−*	2849.68 *	19123.00 *
6/10	INT TEMP FUND	12.36		
	BAL AS OF 6/10/80 19,233.07 **	2739.61−*	2849.68 *	19123.00 *
6/20	CK#14857 JAS R MEANY & ASSOC PREPARATION OF INCOME TAX RETURNS	150.00−		
	BAL AS OF 6/20/80 19,083.07 **	2889.61−*	2849.68 *	19123.00 *
6/24	PRIN CASH TO INCOME CASH FOR TAXES PAID 5-16-80 FROM INCOME SHOULD HAVE BEEN PAID BY PRIN CASH BECAUSE OF THE SALE OF BONDS IN TRUST 3-30-79	2691.00	2691.00−	
6/24	TRANSFER FROM SAVINGS		39.93	39.93−
	BAL AS OF 6/24/80 19,083.07 **	198.61−*	198.61 *	19083.07 *

When discussing transactions in the account ledger, the terms "increase" and "decrease" are used rather than the normal accounting terms "debit" and "credit." For example, the receipt of a dividend would increase income cash, and the purchase of a common stock would increase assets and decrease principal cash. Technically, when looking at the system as a whole, the receipt of the dividend results in a debit to the trust fund's bank account and a credit to the income cash of the individual fiduciary account. The reasoning behind this statement of the entry is that the trust fund bank account is an asset of the trust company's, and the income cash of the individual fiduciary account represents the trust company's liability to the income beneficiary of that account.

When the trust company is a trust department of a bank, all the assets held by the department are offset by liabilities to the beneficiaries of the fiduciary accounts, and none of the assets is reflected in the bank's balance sheet. Only the deposits of the trust department would be included in the bank's balance sheet, the same as any other customer's deposit.

List of Assets

The list of assets, illustrated in Figure 9-2, sets forth the details of the assets held in a particular fiduciary's account. A detailed description of each asset is followed by the trade date or the date the asset came into the fiduciary's control, whichever is applicable, and a lot number. The use of lot numbers allows the fiduciary to identify specific purchases of assets when more than one purchase of an asset has been made.

FIGURE 9-2

40-00305.00 TR A U/A SAMUEL DOUGLAS	LIST OF ASSETS		06/24/80 PAGE 1			
ASSET DESCRIPTION	PAR/SHARES	NET/SHR	COST VALUE	PLG P	R	LOC
05-7235 TEMP FUND T/D 09/27/79 LOT 001	50.0000	100.00	50.00		5	08
10-2113 FED FARM CREDIT BANKS 09.9000% MAT 10/20/80 T/D 04/11/79 LOT 001	9,000.0000	100.00	9,000.00		5	04
10-2114 FED FARM CREDIT BANKS 09.4500% MAT 04/23/80 T/D 04/11/79 LOT 001	10,000.0000	100.00	10,000.00		5	04
22-0862 CITIZENS NATIONAL BANK SAVINGS ACCOUNT 5.75% T/D 04/30/79 LOT 001	33.0700	100.00	33.07		2	01
TOTAL INVESTMENT			19,083.07**			

The total par value is reflected in the case of bonds and the number of shares is shown in the case of stocks. The cost of bonds is shown as the dollar cost per $100 of par value, and the cost per share of stock is shown. The total cost value is given for each asset. The cost value is actual cost of assets purchased by the fiduciary or it is the value established at the time the asset came into the control of the fiduciary if the asset was transferred to the fiduciary. The total cost value of the assets on the list of assets must equal the total assets on the account ledger for the fiduciary account.

The list contains a code designating how the asset is registered and a code designating the location of the asset. Other codes that are useful in managing the assets of the account are sometimes included.

Other Records Produced

As a minimum, the electronic data processing system for a trust company should be able to produce the following trust information;

Trial Balance—The trial balance is a list of all the fiduciary accounts with the accounts grouped according to type of account, such as estates, trusts, agencies, and others. The list shows the account number, name, and the amount of income cash, principal cash, and investments for each account. All amount columns are sub-totaled for each grouping and grand totals are shown.

List Account Assets by Trust—The list of account assets by trust is very much the same as the list of assets shown in Figure 9-2. In some cases, the list of account assets by trusts includes coding for investment restrictions, investment powers, asset retention powers, and the trust officer responsible for the account; however, the foregoing information is generally reflected on an account information sheet that is designed to show all pertinent powers and restrictions set forth in the trust instrument along with information about the account's beneficiaries. The list of account assets by trust may also be expanded to include the market value of the assets listed.

Trust List of Overdrafts—Principal and Income—Every fiduciary account that has an overdraft in either income cash or principal cash appears on the trust list of overdrafts. The account number, name, and the balances of both income cash and principal cash are shown on the list.

Property Master List—The property master list shows each asset held by the trust company. The par value of bonds or number of shares of stock is shown with a unit carrying value, and a total carrying value is shown for each asset.

Holders' List of Each Asset—The holders' list of each asset lists the fiduciary accounts holding each asset in the property master list. The list shows the account number, name, and amount held by par, or shares, whichever is applicable.

Reject Reports—The reject reports list all items that have been rejected by the computer in order that the reasons for the rejections can be determined and the items properly used.

Liabilities—Liabilities are listed by account in the same order as the trial balance. The account number, name, carrying value, and description of the liability are shown.

General Ledger—A complete general ledger for the trust company is processed independently of the other reports produced. Some trust companies produce the general ledger manually, using control figures, and compare the result with the computer output for control purposes. Remember, the general ledger for a trust company may be only control accounts over income cash, principal cash, and investments rather than a formal general ledger.

In addition to the reports listed above, there are numerous other reports that can be generated to assist in the administration of fiduciary accounts and in the investment of funds. For example, a report listing all investment transactions by fiduciary account for a designated period of time could be generated for use by the Trust Investment Committee in its review of investment transactions. Another important report is the portfolio appraisal which is used by the Trust Committee in its periodic review of trust investments. The report lists each investment in the account and its book value, market value, estimated annual income, and yield based on market value. There is also given a summary by type of investment in the account which shows the same information by type of investment.

Once the pertinent data and transactions for a fiduciary account have been entered into the computer system, they can be rearranged and printed out in many different formats for use in managing the account.

Reports to Beneficiaries

The reports produced for beneficiaries will vary from trust company to trust company; however, the reports generally contain the following sections:

Schedule of Transactions—The schedule of transactions is presented in much the same format as the account ledger. The date and a detailed description is given for each transaction. The dollar amounts are shown in columns for income cash, principal cash, and investments.

Summary of Principal Transactions—The summary of principal transactions reflects a summary of the transactions in the principal cash column of the schedule of transactions. The beginning and ending cash balances must be the same as on the schedule of transactions. The transactions are summarized in a reasonable number of categories such as contributions to the account, investment sales, investment purchases, and others.

Summary of Income Transactions—The summary of income transactions reflects a summary of the transactions in the income cash columns of the schedule of transactions. The transactions are summarized in a broader number of categories since total interest and dividend income for each investment is shown in addition to a grand total of interest and dividends.

Schedule of Investments—The schedule of investments provides a detailed description of each investment. The number of shares is shown in the case of stocks and the total par or face value is shown in the case of bonds. The total approximate market value as of the date of the statement is shown for each investment in a column next to the carrying or book value.

Entering Transactions

Transactions are entered into the system by the use of input forms that contain spaces for the various codes used, alpha descriptions, and dollar amounts. The transactions are entered as either increases or decreases to income cash, principal cash, or assets. A transaction may affect only cash, it may affect cash and assets, or it may affect only assets.

Remember, the transactions discussed here are only one side of the actual entry on the trust company's records. Only the records the accountant has to work with are being discussed and not the controls maintained by the trust company.

Cash Transactions

The receipt of income results in an increase in income cash; therefore, the receipt of a dividend on common stock will appear as an increase in income cash on the account ledger. A distribution of income to a beneficiary is a decrease in income cash and it will appear as a decrease in income cash on the account ledger.

Principal cash is increased by the contribution of cash to the account, the receipt of a type of distribution on an asset that is considered principal, and the proceeds from the sale of assets. Disbursements of all types that are chargeable to principal are decreases in principal cash and appear on the account ledger as such.

Asset Transactions

Transactions affecting assets are the contribution of assets to the account, the purchase of an asset, the sale of an asset, the collection of mortgages or other loans carried as assets, amortization of bond premiums, and the collection of accrued interest that was purchased with an investment.

When assets—other than cash—are contributed to a fiduciary account, they are placed on the records of the account as increases in the assets of the account at the appropriate valuation. The transaction will appear as an increase in the assets column on the account ledger.

The purchase of an asset will result in an increase in assets and a decrease in principal cash for the cost of the asset. If accrued interest is purchased with an asset, such as with a bond, it is carried as an asset until the first interest payment date. When the first interest payment is received, the portion attributable to accrued interest purchased is recorded as an increase in principal cash and a decrease in assets, while the remainder is recorded as an increase in income cash.

If a bond is purchased at a premium, the premium should be amortized over the life of the bond—though this is not usually done by an individual fiduciary. The pro-rata portion of the premium attributable to each interest collection is recorded as an increase in principal cash and a decrease in assets. The remainder of the interest collected is recorded as an increase in income cash.

When an asset is sold, it is very unlikely that the proceeds from the sale will equal the book value of the asset. Principal cash is increased by the proceeds from the sale and the assets are decreased by the book value. The gain or loss on the transaction is generally noted in the description column of the account ledger.

Liabilities

In cases where it is desirable to record liabilities in a fiduciary account, they are reflected as negative assets. Transactions involving liabilities will appear in the asset column on the account ledger, and the balances of liabilities are shown on the list of assets as negative amounts.

Distinction Between Principal and Income

The distinction between principal and income is maintained strictly through income cash in the accounting system used by trust companies. The balance in income cash is the amount of income available for distribution to income beneficiaries or for any other disposition called for in the trust instrument.

When investments are made, principal cash is decreased regardless of whether the investment is from income or principal. This transaction results in the principal cash reflecting an overdraft which is offset by the balance in income cash. Many times account ledgers will reflect a balance of income cash equal to an overdraft in principal cash. When this situation exists, the account is fully invested with no funds idle in a checking account.

Interest income added to a savings account is a good example of how this transaction works. When the interest is added to the account, three entries are made:

1. Income cash is increased to reflect the receipt of income.
2. Principal cash is decreased as though principal cash equal to the interest was transferred to the savings account.
3. Assets are increased by the amount of the interest.

The two cash transactions offset each other, and the asset, savings account, is increased by the interest credited. As a result of the entries, income cash includes the interest income on the savings account, and it is available for whatever disposition is proper in accordance with the trust instrument.

Summary

1. The accounting system used by trust companies is designed to account for a large number of trust accounts within a framework of controls over cash transactions and investments of trust assets.

2. The accountant performing a service for a particular trust account will work primarily with the account ledger, list of assets, and reports to beneficiaries generated by the trust company's accounting system.

3. The accounting systems of trust companies generate a multitude of reports used in managing trust accounts.

4. The transactions on the account ledger actually represent only one-half of the accounting entry, and the underlying controls over the system are not apparent to anyone looking at the account ledger.

5. Entries used to record transactions in the account ledger are in terms of increases and decreases rather than debits and credits normally used by accountants.

6. The income cash balance is used to maintain the distinction between principal and income even if some income cash is actually used to purchase investments.

The Fiduciary's Compensation

10

Although the subject of a fiduciary's compensation is not directly related to fiduciary accounting, a brief chapter on this subject should be worthwhile to the fiduciary accountant. Many executors and trustees are likely to be unfamiliar with the basis for arriving at the amount of their compensation and will expect their accountants to be able to give them some information on this subject.

And the subject is an interesting one because of the tremendous variance in the amount the compensation would be—for substantially the same services—from one jurisdiction to another.

Compensation in General

Modern executors and trustees do work for pay, though this was not always so. They have a right to compensation even when it is not granted in the will or trust instrument, but the determination of the amount is not always simple or easy.

A fiduciary's compensation, if not specified in the instrument, is generally fixed by state law and is most often based on the size of the fund being administered. The amount granted by law is known as a fee or a commission.

There is a great diversity in the various state laws regarding these commissions. Some states simply provide for "fair" or "reasonable" compensation, with some of these laws stipulating maximum amounts. In these states the amount allowed might even vary from county to county, depending on the established practices for a particular county or on what a particular probate judge might consider to be "reasonable."

Other states have percentage rates computed on a graduated basis on the size of the fund or on the income. Sometimes lesser rates are allowed on certain types of assets on the theory that the amount of work required with such assets is less than might be required in connection with other types of property, but a higher rate is sometimes permitted where the fiduciary must collect rents and manage real property. Some states also provide for additional compensation for "extraordinary" services.

So it can be seen that only very general rules can be given here on the subject of compensation; the accountant should become familiar with his particular state's laws governing fiduciary fees to be of most help to his fiduciary client in this area.

Executors' Commissions

If the amount of an executor's fee is established in the decedent's will, or if it is fixed by a contract between the testator and his executor, that amount will be allowed by the court. If given in the will, the executor may agree to accept that amount or to accept, instead, the legal amount or refuse the appointment.

If the amount is not fixed, state law controls. In states where the "fair" and "reasonable" rule applies, local practices and guidelines will have been established, and the executor should follow these in arriving at the amount to ask for. He must petition the probate court for the amount, which will either be allowed or scaled down.

In states where a commission base is given in the law, that, of course, governs. But the definition of the commission base also varies from state to state. Some statutes define the commission base as the *gross* estate (the estate tax concept, and therefore not the legal or probate estate) adjusted for such items as life insurance, while others confine the base to items of the *probate* estate on the theory that items that are not part of the legal estate do not require the services of the fiduciary. Specific legacies and devises are often excluded from the commission base; increases and decreases in value during the period of administration are often included in the base.

The legal percentage rates will be applied to the proper base, but if there is any provision for additional compensation for "extraordinary" services, that should not be overlooked; and the executor should also request an additional amount for any out-of-pocket expenses.

As a reminder—an executor's commission is taxable income to the recipient, but a bequest or legacy is not; the comparative tax advantages for estate and income tax purposes should be considered by an executor who is also the residuary legatee. He may find it advantageous to increase his legacy by waiving his fee.

Examples of Executors' Compensation Laws

To better illustrate the ways in which various state laws provide for an executor's fee, extracts from the laws of four different states are given.

First, the Florida law is one that provides for "reasonable" compensation but gives certain criteria for determining just what is reasonable:

Compensation of Personal Representatives and Professionals.

(1) Personal representatives, attorneys, accountants, and appraisers shall be entitled to reasonable compensation. Reasonable compensation shall be based on one or more of the following:

(a) The time and labor required, the novelty and difficulty of the questions involved, and the skill required to perform the service properly.

(b) The likelihood that the acceptance of the particular employment will preclude other employment by the person.

(c) The fee customarily charged in the locality for similar services.

(d) The amount involved and the results obtained.

(e) The time limitations imposed by the circumstances.

(f) The nature and length of the professional relationship with the decedent.

(g) The experience, reputation, diligence, and ability of the person performing the services.

(2) If a will provides for compensation of the personal representative either directly or conditionally and there is no contract with the decedent regarding compensation, he may renounce the provisions and be entitled to reasonable compensation. A personal representative also may renounce his right to all or any part of the compensation. A renunciation may be filed with the court.

(3) If the personal representative is a member of the Florida Bar and has rendered legal services in connection with his official duties, he shall be allowed a fee therefor, determined as provided in subsection (1).

A second example is extracted from the statutes of the state of Kentucky and reads in its entirety as follows:

(1) The compensation of an executor, administrator, or curator, for services as such, may not exceed five percent of the value of the personal estate of the decedent, plus five percent of the income collected by the executor, administrator, or curator for the estate.

(2) Upon proof submitted showing that an executor, administrator, or curator has performed additional services in the administration of the decedent's estate, the court may allow to the executor, administrator, or curator such additional compensation as would be fair and reasonable for the additional services rendered, if the additional services were:

(a) Unusual or extraordinary and not normally incident to the administration of a decedent's estate; or

(b) Performed in connection with real estate or with estate and inheritance taxes claimed against property that is not a part of the decedent's estate but is included in the decedent's estate for the purposes of asserting such taxes.

A statute of this kind would seem to be rather specific and easy to work with, but upon analysis it raises as many questions as it answers. For example, just what is meant by the term "income collected by the executor"? Is it the *gross* cash receipts? Is it the *net* income from the operations? If an estate asset is sold, would the total proceeds be included? If not, would it include just the gain on the sale (or what about a loss)? Local custom and practice might provide the answers to these questions, otherwise the executor should base his claim for compensation on whatever he conscientiously believes to be right.

The New York law provides for determining the amount of an executor's compensation on a sliding rate scale, as follows:

Commissions of Fiduciaries Other Than Trustees.

(1) On the settlement of the account of any fiduciary other than a trustee the court must allow him the reasonable and necessary expenses actually paid by him and if he be an attorney of this state and shall have rendered legal services in connection with his official duties, such compensation for his legal services as shall appear to be just and reasonable, and in addition thereto it must allow to the fiduciary for his services as fiduciary a commission from principal for paying out all sums of money constituting principal at the rate of 1 percent.

(2) In addition to the commission allowed by subdivision 1 hereof an executor shall be entitled to an annual commission at the following rates:

(a) For receiving and paying out all sums of money not exceeding $25,000 at the rate of 4 percent.

(b) For receiving and paying out any additional sums not exceeding $125,000 at the rate of 31/2 percent.

(c) For receiving and paying out any additional sums not exceeding $150,000 at the rate of 3 percent.

(d) For receiving and paying out all sums above $300,000 at the rate of 2 percent.

(2) The value of any property, to be determined in such manner as directed by the court and the increment thereof, received, distributed or delivered, shall be considered as money in computing commissions. But this shall not apply in case of a specific legacy or devise. Whenever any portion of the dividends, interest or rent payable to a fiduciary other than a trustee is required by any law of the United States or other governmental unit to be withheld by the person paying it for income tax purposes, the amount so withheld shall be deemed to have been received and paid out.

(3), (4) not applicable.

(5) If the gross value of the principal of the estate accounted for amounts to $200,000 or more each fiduciary is entitled to the full compensation on principal and income allowed herein to a sole fiduciary unless there be more than 3, in which case the compensation to which 3 would be entitled must be apportioned among them according to the services rendered by them respectively. If the gross value of the principal of the estate accounted for is less than $200,000 but more than $100,000 and there is more than 1 fiduciary the full

compensation for receiving and paying out principal and income allowed herein to a sole fiduciary is allowed to each unless there are more than 2, in which case the commission allowed to two must be apportioned among them according to the services rendered by them respectively. If less than $100,000, the commission to which one sole fiduciary is entitled must be apportioned among the fiduciaries. Where the will provides a specific compensation to a fiduciary other than a trustee he is not entitled to any allowance for his services unless by an instrument filed with the court within 4 months from the date of his letters he renounces the specific compensation.

(6) Where a fiduciary is for any reason entitled or required to collect the rents of and manage real property he shall be allowed and may retain for such services 5 percent of the gross rents collected therefrom in addition to the commissions herein provided, but there shall be only one such additional commission regardless of the number of fiduciaries. In the event there are 2 or more fiduciaries the additional commission herein provided for must be apportioned among them according to the services rendered by them respectively.

California is another state that provides for a sliding fee scale for executors, summarized as follows:

Commissions of executors or administrators and fees for attorneys of either are each computed at the rate of 4% on the first $15,000; 3% on the next $85,000; 2% on the next $900,000; and 1% on all over $1,000,000. A contract with heirs, devisees, or legatees for higher compensation is void, but provisions in the will fixing the compensation of representatives will be enforced. The court may allow additional compensation for extraordinary services.

Trustees' Commissions

A trustee's commission is usually not a very great amount for the work involved. According to Daniel M. Schuyler,

The trustee's job, I think, does not
afford him such a happy lot.

In return for modest fees
he's subject to a constant squeeze.

And written in the trustee's bible
is the rule: "You're always liable."

In view of this how can it be
that anyone would be trustee?

Still, trustees do have a right to compensation for their services, even where not granted in the trust instrument, and the amount of this compensation will be fixed either by the terms of the trust instrument, by contract between the grantor and the trustee, by statute, or by court action.

If there is a contract on compensation, the trustee will be bound by it, and he will be bound by compensation terms in the trust instrument if he did not initially object to them.

Legislation on Trustees' Compensation

Most states have legislation on the allowance of trustee compensation, which will govern in the absence of a contract or terms in the trust instrument. The most common type of law authorizes the court, in its discretion, to allow the trustee "reasonable compensation." The trustee will generally request a specific amount, and the court will grant that amount or whatever lesser amount it deems fair and reasonable.

A few states provide that the trustee is "entitled" to reasonable compensation and give him the power to collect his compensation annually from the trust property without court action.

Still other states have statutes which set forth, in varying degrees of detail, a schedule or scale of commissions or fees that are permitted a trustee. Most of these schedules grant the trustee a graduated percentage of trust income, typically five or six percent on the first $5,000 and a lesser percent on additional brackets. The trouble with income commissions is that they work a hardship on a trustee who holds unproductive or low-yield properties, but most fee schedules meet this problem by awarding additional compensation based on some other criteria, such as commissions on the receipt of corpus (as high as five percent in some jurisdictions) or commissions on the distribution of corpus, either periodically or at the termination of the trust (from one to two-and-a-half percent in various jurisdictions). Another alternative is an annual commission based on the fair market value of the trust corpus. Such commissions are also graduated downward, with a rate of one-half of one percent on the first $50,000 of corpus being a typical maximum rate, with lesser amounts specified in states where a corpus commission is not the principal source of trustee compensation.

But, again, a grantor can override any statutory or judicial compensation arrangement by a contrary direction in the trust instrument; and a binding compensation contract will have the same effect.

Unless otherwise provided by statute or in the trust instrument, a trustee cannot take his compensation until authorized by a court, usually in an accounting proceeding. This rule can, of course, work a financial hardship on trustees, and by lumping the payment of several years' compensation in a single year it can also have unfavorable tax effects on a trustee. So, in recent years, the trend has been toward statutes authorizing trustees to take their commissions annually without court authority.

Corporate Trustees

Corporate trustees tend to avoid fixed-fee arrangements by insisting that the trust instrument include a clause granting them "reasonable compensation" or by specifying other guidelines susceptible of redefinition to meet changing conditions. As an example of a corporate trustee's fee, the Bank of America (San Francisco) generally charges three-fourths of one percent of a trust's assets per year for full management (collecting the income, selling and buying securities, and so on). The fee goes up to one percent if the bank has to manage real estate.

Examples of Trustee Compensation Laws

The majority of the states have laws that simply provide for a reasonable compensation for a trustee, but some have laws that are more specific. It is interesting to note that some states have compensation laws relating to *testamentary* trusts only, not to *inter vivos* trusts, probably on the theory that most living trusts will have built-in compensation arrangements. Several examples of state laws are given here.

The California law is basically one allowing a reasonable compensation, but with a bit more detail than some of the others:

> The trustee of a testamentary trust is entitled to the following compensation: If the instrument specifies an amount, he is entitled to that and no more. If the instrument allows compensation but does not specify the amount, he is entitled to reasonable compensation. If there are several trustees, compensation must be apportioned according to services rendered by each. One becoming an involuntary trustee through his own fault is entitled to no compensation.

The Kentucky law is quite a bit more specific, and it reads as follows:

> **(1)** Trustees of estates shall receive for their services as such a commission of five percent of the income collected by them, payable as the income is collected. They shall also receive an annual commission of one-fifth of one percent of the fair value of the real and personal estate in the care of the fiduciary, or, at the option of the fiduciary and in lieu of the annual commission on principal, a commission which shall not exceed five percent of the fair value of the principal distributed, payable at the time the principal is distributed. In the absence of some provision, agreement, or direction to the contrary, the commission on income shall be paid out of the income from the estate, and the commission on principal shall be paid out of the principal of the estate.

> **(2)** However, upon proof submitted showing that the fiduciary has performed additional service in the handling of the estate in his care, which has been unusual or extraordinary and not normally incident to the care and man-

agement of an estate, the court may allow to the fiduciary such additional compensation as is fair and reasonable for the additional services rendered. This additional compensation shall be payable out of principal or income, or part out of principal and part out of income, as the court directs.

A summary of the law of Hawaii regarding the compensation of a trustee is as follows:

Of all money and property received as trust income, the trustee is allowed 7% commission for the first $5,000 and 5% commission for all over $5,000 payable as income is received, but not more often than once a year. On principal, commissions are as follows: 1% on value at the inception of the trust, payable at such inception out of principal; 1/10 of 1% on value at the end of each year; 1% on value of all or any part of the estate on final distribution thereof, payable at the termination of the trust out of principal; 21/2 % on cash principal received after inception of the trust, payable at the time of receipt out of principal; 21/2% on final payment of any cash principal prior to the termination of the trust, payable at the time of such final payment out of principal. Further allowance may be made by the court for special services, but a contract for a higher compensation between the trustee and beneficiary is void.

The New York law is another which goes into somewhat more detail in the treatment of trustee commissions, summarized as follows:

For inter vivos or testamentary trusts coming into existence after August 31, 1956, annual commissions are payable, based on value of principal at the end of period, of $7 per $1,000 on first $300,000 at end of period, $3.75 per $1,000 on the next $500,000 of principal and $2.50 per $1,000 on balance of principal. Commissions for paying out principal are 1%. Commissions on actual income are 2% of the first $2,500 and 1% of balance payable at time of distribution.

If principal amounts to $200,000 or more each trustee is entitled to full compensation unless there are more than three, in which case compensation to which three are entitled is to be apportioned. If principal amounts to $100,000 or more and less than $200,000 each trustee is entitled to full compensation unless there are more than two, in which case compensation to which two are entitled must be apportioned. If principal is less than $100,000 and there is more than one trustee, full compensation to which a sole trustee is entitled is to be apportioned.

When required to collect rents and manage real property, a trustee is allowed 6% of rents collected in addition to commissions.

Summary

To summarize the method of determining the amount of a fiduciary's commission:

1. If the amount of an executor's fee is spelled out in the will, this establishes the compensation and the court will approve it.

2. If the amount of a trustee's fee is specified in the trust instrument or if there is a contract between the grantor and the trustee, the amount will almost invariably be approved by the court.

3. If no amount is stipulated by the testator or grantor, state law must be consulted for the proper way of computing the compensation of an executor or trustee.

4. A number of states have fee schedules for executors, usually providing for a certain percentage, or percentages, of the gross estate and of the estate's income; other states simply provide for "reasonable" compensation, in which case the time and labor required, the customary compensation for similar services in the locality, the amount of property involved, and other such guidelines must be considered in arriving at the amount.

5. A majority of the states do not have very specific laws regarding a trustee's fee but say that it must be a reasonable and fair amount; other states do have more specific fee schedules for trustees.

6. Most of the states provide for additional compensation, over and above those allowed by the fee schedules, for the performance of additional and extraordinary duties by an executor or a trustee.

Glossary

Abatement. The reduction or total elimination of a legacy because the assets of the estate are insufficient to make payment. For example, if the debts and administration expenses, other legacies, and devises exhaust the assets of the estate, the residuary legacies will abate.

Account of Proceedings. A detailed statement of the fiduciary's acts and proceedings in connection with the administration of an estate or a trust.

Ademption. If the property bequeathed in a specific legacy is disposed of during the lifetime of the testator, the legacy will not be paid. It will have been adeemed.

Administration. The collection and management of a decedent's assets, the payment of his debts, and the distribution of any assets remaining; also, the management of the assets of a trust.

Administration Expenses. Fiduciary commissions, attorneys' fees, accountants' fees, and other expenses of administering an estate or a trust.

Administrator. One named by a court rather than by a will to take charge of the assets of a decedent and to dispose of them in accordance with the law or ruling of the court.

Administratrix. A woman named by a court to administer an estate.

Advancement. The testator may set forth legacies in his will, and then during his lifetime make transfers to the prospective legatees. Whether such transfers should reduce the legacies will be determined from statements to that effect in the will itself, or in the absence of such statements, by state law. Such diminishment of legacies is called the "doctrine of advancement."

Alternate Executor. A person named to serve as executor in the event the person first named is unable or unwilling to serve.

Alternate Trustee. A person named to serve as trustee in the event the person first named is unable or unwilling to serve.

Alternate Value. For estate tax purposes, the value of the gross estate six months after the date of a decedent's death.

Ancillary. Subordinate; auxiliary; as "ancillary administration," meaning an auxiliary administration required in other states than the one in which the decedent had his residence.

Appraise. To establish cost or value by systematic procedures that include physical examination, pricing, and often engineering estimates.

Appraiser. One who appraises property, such as the property in a decedent's estate.

Beneficial Interest. An interest in property held in trust, as distinguished from legal ownership.

Beneficiary. One who is lawfully entitled to the proceeds of property, the title to which is vested in another such as in an executor or a trustee.

Bequest. A gift of property by will; specifically, a gift of personal property rather than real estate; a legacy.

Charge and Discharge Statement. A tabular summary prepared for an executor, trustee, or other fiduciary, accounting for the principal and income for which he has been responsible and constituting a part of an interim or final report on his activities.

Codicil. A written change in, or addition to, a will.

Commission. The compensation provided by law for a fiduciary.

Corpus. The property comprising the gross estate of a decedent; the property comprising the fund which has been set aside in trust, or from which income is expected to accrue; principal.

Creator. The person who establishes a trust, either while alive or through will on death; grantor; settlor.

Cy-Pres Doctrine. A bequest or devise to a charitable organization may be impossible of fulfillment because of a change of circumstances since execution of the will. For example, the legatee organization may no longer exist. If the supervisory court believes that the testator's intent is clear, the legacy may be paid to a substitute, equivalent legatee. If so, the court has invoked the "cy-pres doctrine," which is an attempt to fulfill the testator's intention as nearly as possible; applies only to charitable bequests and devises.

Decedent. A person who has died.

Demonstrative Legacy. A bequest of a sum certain in money, which stipulates the source from which the amount is to be paid. In the event that the source does not contain sufficient funds to satisfy the legacy, it will be paid from the general funds of the estate.

Devise. The disposition of real estate by will.

Devisee. One who receives real estate by will.

Descent. The disposition of the real property of an intestate person.

Distribution, Law of. The apportionment and disposition, by authority of a court, of the balance of an intestate's personal property after payment of debts and costs.

Domicile. That place which is a person's permanent home and to which, whenever he is absent, he has the intention of returning.

Donee. The recipient of a gift.

Donor. For gift tax purposes, the person who makes a gift.

Estate Tax. The tax levied on the transfer of property as a result of death.

Executor. A person named in a will as the fiduciary who is to take charge of the deceased's estate and administer or dispose of it as directed in the will.

Executrix. A woman named in a will to serve as the fiduciary in charge of the deceased's property.

Fiduciary. Any person responsible for the custody or administration, or both, of property belonging to another; as, a trustee, executor, or administrator.

Fiduciary Income Tax Return. The income tax return filed by the fiduciary of an estate or a trust, Form 1041.

General Legacy. A monetary bequest, payable out of the general assets of an estate.

Gift. The transfer of property from one individual to another without consideration.

Gift Tax. The federal tax levied on the transfer of property by inter-vivos gift.

Grantor. The person who established a trust; creator; settlor.

Grantor Trust. A trust which fails to meet certain income tax rules and the property of which is, therefore, considered to be still owned by the grantor for income tax purposes.

Gross Estate. The value of the decedent's assets and rights for estate tax purposes.

Heir. One who on the death of another becomes entitled by operation of law to succeed to the deceased person's estate; anyone inheriting from a deceased person.

Income. The earnings, gains or profits arising from the productive investment or use of the property constituting the principal or capital of an estate or fund.

Income Beneficiary. The person entitled to the income from property in trust, as contrasted with a principal beneficiary, who will receive the property itself.

Inheritance. The property received from a deceased person, by succession or by will; strictly, property received by descent rather than by devise.

Inheritance Tax. A tax levied by various states against each share of property inherited from a decedent.

Intestate. A person who dies without having a valid will in force.

Inter-Vivos Trust. A trust created between living persons, as contrasted with a testamentary trust.

Irrevocable Trust. A trust that cannot be set aside by its creator.

Joint Tenant. Any one of two or more persons who together own an item of real or personal property, whereby upon the death of any one of them his interest passes to the other without becoming a part of his administrable estate.

Lapsed Legacy. A bequest that is not paid, generally falling into the residue, because the beneficiary named in the will predeceased the testator. However, state law may dictate, where a close family relationship existed between testator and beneficiary, that the family of the beneficiary shall receive the legacy in his stead.

Legacy. A gift of personal property by will. A general legacy is one to be paid from the general assets of the testator; a specific legacy is one involving a specified sum of money or personal property; and a residual legacy is the gift of the balance of a testator's estate after payment of debts and costs and other expenses.

Legatee. A person who receives a legacy.

Letters Testamentary. A court order admitting a will to probate and approving and giving authority to the person named as executor.

Letters of Administration. A court order appointing and giving authority to the person selected to be the administrator of an intestate's estate.

Life Estate. The title of the interest owned by the life tenant; income beneficiary.

Life Tenant. One who has a life estate, the right to receive the income from property or use of the property for his lifetime. More generally, however, one may be an income beneficiary of a trust for a period of years or until reaching a specified age or until the happening of an event.

Living Trust. A trust created by a living person, to take effect before his death; an inter-vivos trust.

Marital Deduction. The deduction allowed for estate tax and for gift tax purposes for qualifying property transferred to the spouse.

Marital Deduction Trust. A testamentary trust which meets certain tax requirements so that its property may qualify for the marital deduction.

Personal Property. Property of a temporary and movable character, as contrasted with real property.

Power of Appointment. A power given to the possessor by another person, which authorizes him to control, with certain limitations, the ultimate disposition of the property subject to the power.

Power of Invasion. The power to withdraw principal from a trust, which power is usually designed to make up to the beneficiary any insufficiency in the income intended for his support. The power may be limited by a standard, such as the circumstances under which invasion is permitted, or by a dollar limitation.

Principal. The original amount of an estate's property, or of the property of a trust fund, together with accretions which may, but usually do not, include income; corpus.

Principal Beneficiary. The person to whom the property constituting the principal of a trust will go upon termination of the trust.

Probate. The formal, legal proving of a will and its acceptance by the court having jurisdiction over the administration of estates.

Probate Court. The court which exercises judicial authority in all matters relating to decedents' estates.

Real Property. Land and land improvements, including buildings and appurtenances.

Remainderman. One entitled to the corpus or principal of a trust upon the expiration of a prior estate, such as a life tenancy; a principal beneficiary.

Renunciation. The refusal by a legatee or devisee to accept a testamentary disposition or power. A renounced specific or general legacy falls into the residue; a renounced residuary legacy passes under the state law on intestacy.

Residuary Estate. The estate of a decedent remaining after the payment of all administration and funeral expenses, debts, taxes, charges, and legacies.

Residuary Legacy. A bequest of the balance, or residue, of personalty remaining after payment of debts, funeral and administration expenses, and all other types of legacies and devises.

Residuary Legatee. One entitled to receive the balance of an estate after specific bequests, taxes, and other liabilities have been satisfied.

Reversion. The return to the grantor of a trust of the principal of the trust after a period during which a beneficiary has received the income from, or use of, the property.

Revocable Trust. A trust terminable at the pleasure of or under certain conditions by its creator.

Settlor. The person who makes a gift to an inter-vivos trust; grantor.

Short-Term Trust. A trust established to be irrevocable for a period of at least ten years; also known as a "Clifford" trust.

Specific Legacy. A bequest of personal property which is described with particularity in the will. The bequest can be satisfied only by the described property, so if the property is not in the estate as of the date of death the legacy is adeemed.

Successor Trustee. One named to assume the duties of trustee upon the death or disqualification of the original trustee.

Taxable Income. For income tax purposes, the excess of the total income of an estate or a trust over the distribution deduction and all other deductions, including the exemption.

Tenancy in Common. Ownership of property by two or more persons, with each having a different degree of interest; when one of the tenants dies, his interest passes to his beneficiaries, not to his fellow tenants.

Tenancy, Joint. Ownership by two or more persons of the same property, at the same time, by the same conveyance, with each having the same degree of interest and the same right of undivided possession as the others. It is distinguished by the automatic passage of one tenant's interest to the others by survivorship and it can be terminated by any one tenant's conveyance of his interest.

Tenancy by the Entirety. Similar to a joint tenancy, except that it applies only to real property, the joint tenants must be husband and wife, and neither can terminate the tenancy without the consent of the other while he or she is alive. Upon the death of one tenant, entire ownership of the property automatically passes to the other.

Testamentary Trust. A trust created by a person's will, to go into effect after his death.

Testamentary. Pertaining to a testator or his estate.

Testate. Having made a valid will before decease which is in effect at death.

Testator. One who makes a will.

Totten Trust. A revocable trust created by the deposit by one person of his own money in his own name as a trustee for another.

Trust. A right, enforceable in courts of equity, to the beneficial enjoyment of property, the legal title to which is in another. The person creating the trust is the creator, settlor, grantor, or donor; the holder of the legal title is the trustee; and the holder of the beneficial interest is the beneficiary.

Trust Fund. A fund held by one person, the trustee, for the benefit of another, pursuant to the provisions of a formal trust instrument.

Trustee. The fiduciary nominated by the testator or settlor or appointed by the court to administer the trust property.

Trustor. A person who established a trust; creator; grantor.

Trust Instrument. A written document reciting the terms and conditions under which property placed in trust shall be administered.

Will. A document prepared by a natural person in contemplation of death and containing instructions for the disposition of his property.

Appendix

APPENDIX One

Uniform Trustees' Powers Act*

Sec.

1. Definitions.
2. Powers of Trustee Conferred by Trust or by Law.
3. Powers of Trustees Conferred by this Act.
4. Trustee's Office Not Transferable.
5. Power of Court to Permit Deviation or to Approve Transactions Involving Conflict of Interest.
6. Powers Exercisable by Joint Trustees Liability.
7. Third Persons Protected in Dealing with Trustee.
8. Application of Act.
9. Uniformity of Interpretation.
10. Short Title.

Section 1. *(Definitions.)* As used in this Act:

(1) "trust" means an express trust created by a trust instrument, including a will, whereby a trustee has the duty to administer a trust asset for the benefit of a named or otherwise described income or principal beneficiary, or both; "trust" does not include a resulting or constructive trust, a business trust which provides for certificates to be issued to the beneficiary, an investment trust, a voting trust, a security instrument, a trust created by the judgment or decree of a court, a liquidation trust, or a trust for the primary purpose of paying dividends, interest, interest coupons, salaries, wages, pensions or profits, or employee benefits of any kind, an instrument wherein a person is nominee or escrowee for another, a trust

---

*Drafted for the National Conference of Commissioners on Uniform State Laws by Charles Horowitz. Approved 1964. Adopted in Florida, Idaho, Kansas, Kentucky, Mississippi, Montana, New Hampshire, Oregon, Utah, Wyoming.

created in deposits in any financial institution, or other trust the nature of which does not admit of general trust administration;

(2) "trustee" means an original, added, or successor trustee;

(3) "prudent man" means a trustee whose exercise of trust powers is reasonable and equitable in view of the interests of income or principal beneficiaries, or both, and in view of the manner in which men of ordinary prudence, diligence, discretion, and judgment would act in the management of their own affairs.

Section 2. *(Powers of Trustee Conferred by Trust or by Law.)* (a) The trustee has all powers conferred upon him by the provisions of this Act unless limited in the trust instrument [and except as is otherwise provided in _____].

(b) An instrument which is not a trust under section 1(1) may incorporate any part of this Act by reference.

Section 3. *(Powers of Trustees Conferred by this Act.)*

(a) From time of creation of the trust until final distribution of the assets of the trust, a trustee has the power to perform, without court authorization, every act which a prudent man would perform for the purposes of the trust including but not limited to the powers specified in subsection (c).

(b) In the exercise of his powers including the powers granted by this Act, a trustee has a duty to act with due regard to his obligation as a fiduciary, including a duty not to exercise any power under this Act in such a way as to deprive the trust of an otherwise available tax exemption, deduction, or credit for tax purposes or deprive a donor of a trust asset of a tax exemption, deduction, or credit or operate to impose a tax upon a donor or other person as owner of any portion of the trust. "Tax" includes, but is not limited to, any federal, state, or local income, gift, estate, or inheritance tax.

(c) A trustee has the power, subject to subsections (a) and (b):

(1) to collect, hold, and retain trust assets received from a trustor until, in the judgment of the trustee, disposition of the assets should be made; and the assets may be retained even though they include an asset in which the trustee is personally interested;

(2) to receive additions to the assets of the trust;

(3) to continue or participate in the operation of any business or other enterprise, and to effect incorporation, dissolution, or other change in the form of the organization of the business or enterprise;

(4) to acquire an undivided interest in a trust asset in which the trustee, in any trust capacity, holds an undivided interest;

(5) to invest and reinvest trust assets in accordance with the provisions of the trust or as provided by law;

(6) to deposit trust funds in a bank, including a bank operated by the trustee;

(7) to acquire or dispose of an asset, for cash or on credit, at public or private sale; and to manage, develop, improve, exchange, partition, change the character of, or abandon a trust asset or any interest therein; and to encumber, mortgage, or pledge a trust asset for a term within or extending beyond the term of the trust, in connection with the exercise of any power vested in the trustee;

(8) to make ordinary or extraordinary repairs or alterations in buildings or other structures, to demolish any improvements, to raze existing or erect new party walls or buildings;

(9) to subdivide, develop, or dedicate land to public use; or to make or obtain the vacation of plats and adjust boundaries; or to adjust differences in valuation on exchange or partition by giving or receiving consideration; or to dedicate easements to public use without consideration;

(10) to enter for any purpose into a lease as lessor or lessee with or without option to purchase or renew for a term within or extending beyond the term of the trust;

(11) to enter into a lease or arrangement for exploration and removal of minerals or other natural resources or enter into a pooling or unitization agreement;

(12) to grant an option involving disposition of a trust asset, or to take an option for the acquisition of any asset;

(13) to vote a security, in person or by general or limited proxy;

(14) to pay calls, assessments, and any other sums chargeable or accruing against or on account of securities;

(15) to sell or exercise stock subscription or conversion rights; to consent, directly or through a committee or other agent, to the reorganization, consolidation, merger, dissolution, or liquidation of a corporation or other business enterprise;

(16) to hold a security in the name of a nominee or in other form without disclosure of the trust, so that title to the security may pass by delivery, but the trustee is liable for any act of the nominee in connection with the stock so held;

(17) to insure the assets of the trust against damage or loss, and the trustee against liability with respect to third persons;

(18) to borrow money to be repaid from trust assets or otherwise; to advance money for the protection of the trust, and for all expenses, losses, and liabilities sustained in the administration of the trust or because of the holding or ownership of any trust assets, for which advances with any interest the trustee has a lien on the trust assets as against the beneficiary;

(19) to pay or contest any claim; to settle a claim by or against the trust by compromise, arbitration, or otherwise; and to release, in whole or in part, any claim belonging to the trust to the extent that the claim is uncollectible;

(20) to pay taxes, assessments, compensation of the trustee, and other expenses incurred in the collection, care, administration, and protection of the trust;

(21) to allocate items of income or expense to either trust income or principal, as provided by law, including creation of reserves out of income for depreciation, obsolescence, or amortization, or for depletion in mineral or timber properties;

(22) to pay any sum distributable to a beneficiary under legal disability, without liability to the trustee, by paying the sum to the beneficiary or by paying the sum for the use of the beneficiary either to a legal representative appointed by the court, or if none, to a relative;

(23) to effect distribution of property and money in divided or undivided interests and to adjust resulting differences in valuation;

(24) to employ persons, including attorneys, auditors, investment advisors, or agents, even if they are associated with the trustee, to advise or assist the trustee in the performance of his administrative duties; to act without independent investigation upon their recommendations; and instead of acting personally, to employ one or more agents to perform any act of administration, whether or not discretionary;

(25) to prosecute or defend actions, claims, or proceedings for the protection of trust assets and of the trustee in the performance of his duties;

(26) to execute and deliver all instruments which will accomplish or facilitate the exercise of the powers vested in the trustee.

Section 4. *(Trustee's Office Not Transferable.)* The trustee shall not transfer his office to another or delegate the entire administration of the trust to a cotrustee or another.

Section 5. *(Power of Court to Permit Deviation or to Approve Transactions Involving Conflict of Interest.)*

(a) This Act does not affect the power of a court of competent jurisdiction for cause shown and upon petition of the trustee or affected beneficiary and upon appropriate notice to the affected parties to relieve a trustee from any restrictions on his power that would otherwise be placed upon him by the trust or by this Act.

(b) If the duty of the trustee and his individual interest or his interest as trustee of another trust, conflict in the exercise of a trust power, the power may be exercised only by court authorization (except as provided in sections 3(c) (1), (4), (6), (18), and (24)) upon petition of the trustee. Under this section, personal profit or advantage to an affiliated or subsidiary company or association is personal profit to any corporate trustee.

Section 6. *(Powers Exercisable by Joint Trustees Liability.)* (a) Any power vested in 3 or more trustees may be exercised by a majority, but a trustee who has not joined in exercising a power is not liable to the beneficiaries or to others for the consequences of the exercise; and a dissenting trustee is not liable for the consequences of an act in which he joins at the direction of the majority of the trustees, if he expressed his dissent in writing to any of his cotrustees at or before the time of the joinder.

(b) If 2 or more trustees are appointed to perform a trust, and if any of them is unable or refuses to accept the appointment, or, having accepted, ceases to be a trustee, the surviving or remaining trustees shall perform the trust and succeed to all the powers, duties, and discretionary authority given to the trustees jointly.

(c) This section does not excuse a cotrustee from liability for failure either to participate in the administration of the trust or to attempt to prevent a breach of trust.

Section 7. *(Third Persons Protected in Dealing with Trustee.)* With respect to a third person dealing with a trustee or assisting a trustee in the conduct of a transaction, the existence of trust powers and their proper exercise by the trustee may be assumed without inquiry. The third person is not bound to inquire whether the trustee has power to act or is properly exercising the power; and a third person, without actual knowledge that the trustee is exceeding his powers or improperly exercising them, is fully protected in dealing with the trustee as if the trustee possessed and properly exercised the powers he purports to exercise. A third person is not bound to assure the proper application of trust assets paid or delivered to the trustee.

Section 8. *(Application of Act.)* Except as specifically provided in the trust, the provisions of this Act apply to any trust established [before or] after the effective date of this Act and to any trust asset acquired by the trustee [before or] after the effective date of this Act.

Section 9. *(Uniformity of Interpretation.)* This Act shall be construed to effectuate its general purpose to make uniform the law of those states which enact it.

Section 10. *(Short Title.)* This Act may be cited as the "Uniform Trustees' Powers Act."

APPENDIX **Two**

Uniform Fiduciaries Act*

Sec.

1. *Definition of Terms:*—(1) In this act unless the context or subject matter otherwise requires:

"Bank" includes any person or association of persons, whether incorporated or not, carrying on the business of banking.

---

* Drafted for the National Conference of Commissioners on Uniform State Laws by Austin W. Scott. Approved 1922. Adopted in Alabama, Arizona, Colorado, District of Columbia, Hawaii, Idaho, Illinois, Indiana, Louisiana, Maryland, Minnesota, Missouri, Nevada, New Jersey, New York, North Carolina, Ohio, Pennsylvania, Rhode Island, South Dakota, Tennessee, Utah, Virgin Islands, Wisconsin, Wyoming.

"Fiduciary" includes a trustee under any trust, expressed, implied, resulting or constructive, executor, administrator, guardian, conservator, curator, receiver, trustee in bankruptcy, assignee for the benefit of creditors, partner, agent, officer of a corporation, public or private, public officer, or any other person acting in a fiduciary capacity for any person, trust or estate.

"Person" includes a corporation, partnership, or other association, or two or more persons having a joint or common interest.

"Principal" includes any person to whom a fiduciary as such owes an obligation.

(2) A thing is done "in good faith" within the meaning of this act, when it is in fact done honestly, whether it be done negligently or not. [Amended in several states.]

2. *Application of Payments Made to Fiduciaries.*—A person who in good faith pays or transfers to a fiduciary any money or other property which the fiduciary as such is authorized to receive, is not responsible for the proper application thereof by the fiduciary; and any right or title acquired from the fiduciary in consideration of such payment or transfer is not invalid in consequence of a misapplication by the fiduciary.

3. *Registration of Transfer of Securities Held by Fiduciaries.*—If a fiduciary in whose name are registered any shares of stock, bonds or other securities of any corporation, public or private, or company or other association, or of any trust, transfers the same, such corporation or company or other association, or any of the managers of the trust, or its or their transfer agent, is not bound to inquire whether the fiduciary is committing a breach of his obligation as fiduciary in making the transfer, or to see to the performance of the fiduciary obligation, and is liable for registering such transfer only where registration of the transfer is made with actual knowledge that the fiduciary is committing a breach of his obligation as fiduciary in making the transfer, or with knowledge of such facts that the action in registering the transfer amounts to bad faith. [Omitted or repealed in most states.]

4. *Transfer of Negotiable Instrument by Fiduciary.*—If any negotiable instrument payable or indorsed to a fiduciary as such is indorsed by the fiduciary, or if any negotiable instrument payable or indorsed to his principal is indorsed by a fiduciary empowered to indorse such instrument on behalf of his principal, the indorsee is not bound to inquire whether the fiduciary is committing a breach of his obligation as fiduciary in indorsing or delivering the instrument, and is not chargeable with notice that the fiduciary is committing a breach of his obligation as fiduciary unless he takes the instrument with actual knowledge of such breach or with knowledge of such facts that his action in taking the instrument amounts to bad faith. If, however, such instrument is transferred by the fiduciary in payment of or as security for a personal debt of the fiduciary to the actual knowledge of the creditor, or is transferred in any transaction known by the transferee to be for the personal benefit of the fiduciary, the creditor or other transferee is liable to the principal if the fiduciary in fact commits a breach of his obligation as fiduciary in transferring the instrument. [Repealed in several states.]

5. *Check Drawn by Fiduciary Payable to Third Person.*—If a check or other bill of exchange is drawn by a fiduciary as such, or in the name of his principal by a fiduciary empowered to draw such instrument in the name of his principal, the payee is not bound to inquire whether the fiduciary is committing a breach of his obligation as fiduciary in drawing or delivering the instrument, and is not chargeable with notice that the fiduciary is committing a breach of his obligation as fiduciary unless he takes the instrument with actual knowledge of such breach or with knowledge of such facts that his action in taking the instrument amounts to bad faith. If, however, such instrument is payable to a personal creditor of the fiduciary and delivered to the creditor in payment of or as security for a personal debt of the fiduciary to the actual knowledge of the creditor, or is drawn and delivered in any transaction known by the payee to be for the personal benefit of the fiduciary, the creditor or other payee is liable to the principal if the fiduciary in fact commits a breach of his obligation as fiduciary in drawing or delivering the instrument. [Repealed in several states.]

6. *Check Drawn by and Payable to Fiduciary.*—If a check or other bill of exchange is drawn by a fiduciary as such or in the name of his principal by a fiduciary empowered to draw such instrument in the name of his principal, payable to the fiduciary personally, or payable to a third person and by him transferred to the fiduciary, and is thereafter transferred by the fiduciary, whether in payment of a personal debt of the fiduciary or otherwise, the transferee is not bound to inquire whether the fiduciary is committing a breach of his obligation as fiduciary in transferring the instrument, and is not chargeable with notice that the fiduciary is committing a breach of his obligation as fiduciary unless he takes the instrument with actual knowledge of such breach or with knowledge of such facts that his action in taking the instrument amounts to bad faith. [Repealed or amended in several states.]

7. *Deposit in Name of Fiduciary as Such.*—If a deposit is made in a bank to the credit of a fiduciary as such, the bank is authorized to pay the amount of the deposit or any part thereof upon the check of the fiduciary, signed with the name in which such deposit is entered, without being liable to the principal, unless the bank pays the check with actual knowledge that the fiduciary is committing a breach of his obligation as fiduciary in drawing the check or with knowledge of such facts that its action in paying the check amounts to bad faith. If, however, such a check is payable to the drawee bank and is delivered to it in payment of or as security for a personal debt of the fiduciary to it, the bank is liable to the principal if the fiduciary in fact commits a breach of his obligation as fiduciary in drawing or delivering the check. [Amended in several states.]

8. *Deposit in Name of Principal.*—If a check is drawn upon the account of his principal in a bank by a fiduciary who is empowered to draw checks upon his principal's account, the bank is authorized to pay such check without being liable to the principal, unless the bank pays the check with actual knowledge that the fiduciary is committing a breach of his obligation as fiduciary in drawing such check or with knowledge of such facts that its action in paying the check amounts to bad faith. If, however, such a check is payable to the drawee bank and is delivered to it in payment of or as security for a personal debt of the fiduciary to it, the bank is liable to the principal if the fiduciary in fact commits a breach of his obligation as fiduciary in drawing or delivering the check. [Omitted or amended in several states.]

9. *Deposit in Fiduciary's Personal Account.*—If a fiduciary makes a deposit in a bank to his personal credit of checks drawn by him upon an account in his own name as fiduciary, or of checks payable to him as fiduciary, or of checks drawn by him upon an account in the name of his principal if he is empowered to draw checks thereon, or of checks payable to his principal and indorsed by him, if he is empowered to indorse such checks, or if he otherwise makes a deposit of funds held by him as fiduciary, the bank receiving such deposit is not bound to inquire whether the fiduciary is committing thereby a breach of his obligation as fiduciary; and the bank is authorized to pay the amount of the deposit or any part thereof upon the personal check of the fiduciary without being liable to the principal unless the bank receives the deposit or pays the check with actual knowledge that the fiduciary is committing a breach of his obligation as fiduciary in making such deposit or in drawing such check, or with knowledge of such facts that its action in receiving the deposit or paying the check amounts to bad faith.

10. *Deposit in Names of Two or More Trustees.*—When a deposit is made in a bank in the name of two or more persons as trustees and a check is drawn upon the trust account by any trustee or trustees authorized by the other trustee or trustees to draw checks upon the trust account, neither the payee nor other holder nor the bank is bound to inquire whether it is a breach of trust to authorize such trustee or trustees to draw checks upon the trust account, and is not liable unless the circumstances be such that the action of the payee or other holder or the bank amounts to bad faith. [Omitted or amended in several states.]

11. *Act Not Retroactive.*—The provisions of this act shall not apply to transactions taking place prior to the time when it takes effect. [Omitted in several states.]

12. *Cases Not Provided for in Act.*—In any case not provided for in this act the rules of law and equity, including the law merchant and those rules of law and equity relating to trusts, agency, negotiable instruments and banking, shall continue to apply. [Omitted in several states.]

13. *Uniformity of Interpretation.*—This act shall be so interpreted and construed as to effectuate its general purpose to make uniform the law of those states which enact it.

14. *Short Title.*—This act may be cited as the Uniform Fiduciaries Act.

15. *Inconsistent Laws Repealed.*—All acts or parts of acts inconsistent with this act are hereby repealed.

16. *Time of Taking Effect.*—This act shall take effect [   ].

APPENDIX **Three**

Uniform Principal and Income Act*

Sec.

Section 1. *(Definition of terms.)* "Principal" as used in this act means any realty or personalty which has been so set aside or limited by the owner thereof or a person thereto legally empowered that it and any substitutions for it are eventually to be conveyed, delivered or paid to a person, while the return therefrom or

---

*Drafted for the National Conference of Commissioners on Uniform State Laws by Charles E. Clark. Approved 1931. In force in Alabama, Arizona, Colorado, Connecticut, Illinois, Kentucky, Montana, Oklahoma, Pennsylvania, Tennessee, Texas, Virginia, Vermont, West Virginia.

use thereof or any part of such return or use is in the meantime to be taken or received by or held for accumulation for the same or another person;

"Income" as used in this act means the return derived from principal;

"Tenant" as used in this act means the person to whom income is presently or currently payable, or for whom it is accumulated or who is entitled to the beneficial use of the principal presently and for a time prior to its distribution;

"Remainderman" as used in this act means the person ultimately entitled to the principal, whether named or designated by the terms of the transaction by which the principal was established or determined by operation of law;

"Trustee" as used in this act includes the original trustee of any trust to which the principal may be subject and also any succeeding or added trustee. [Amended in several states.]

Section 2. *(Application of the Act—Powers of Settlor.)* This act shall govern the ascertainment of income and principal, and the apportionment of receipts and expenses between tenants and remaindermen, in all cases where a principal has been established with or, unless otherwise stated hereinafter, without the interposition of a trust; except that in the establishment of the principal provision may be made touching all matters covered by this act, and the person establishing the principal may himself direct the manner of ascertainment of income and principal and the apportionment of receipts and expenses or grant discretion to the trustee or other person to do so, and such provision and direction, where not otherwise contrary to law, shall control notwithstanding this act. [Amended in several states.]

Section 3. *(Income and Principal—Disposition.)*

(1) All receipts of money or other property paid or delivered as rent of realty or hire of personalty or dividends on corporate shares payable other than in shares of the corporation itself, or interest on money loaned, or interest on or the rental or use value of property wrongfully withheld or tortiously damaged, or otherwise in return for the use of principal, shall be deemed income unless otherwise expressly provided in this act.

(2) All receipts of money or other property paid or delivered as the consideration for the sale or other transfer, not a leasing or letting, of property forming a part of the principal, or as a repayment of loans, or in liquidation of the assets of a corporation, or as the proceeds of property taken on eminent domain proceedings where separate awards to tenant and remainderman are not made, or as proceeds of insurance upon property forming a part of the principal except where such insurance has been issued for the benefit of either tenant or remainderman alone, or otherwise as a refund or replacement or change in form of principal, shall be deemed principal unless otherwise expressly provided in this act. Any profit or loss resulting upon any change in form of principal shall enure to or fall upon principal.

(3) All income after payment of expenses properly chargeable to it shall be paid or delivered to the tenant or retained by him if already in his possession or held for accumulation where legally so directed by the terms of the transaction by which the principal was established; while the principal shall be held for ultimate distribution as determined by the terms of the transaction by which it was established or by law. [Amended in several states.]

Section 4. *(Apportionment of Income.)* Whenever a tenant shall have the right to income from periodic payments, which shall include rent, interest on loans, and annuities, but shall not include dividends on corporate shares, and such right shall cease and determine by death or in any other manner at a time other than the date when such periodic payments should be paid, he or his personal representative shall be entitled to that portion of any such income next payable which amounts to the same percentage thereof as the time elapsed from the last due date of such periodic payments to and including the day of the determination of his right is of the total period during which such income would normally accrue. The remaining income shall be paid to the person next entitled to income by the terms of the transaction by which the principal was established. But no action shall be brought by the trustee or tenant to recover such apportioned income or any portion thereof until after the day on which it would have become due to the tenant but for the determination of the right of the tenant entitled thereto. The provisions of this section shall apply whether an ultimate remainderman is specifically named or not. Likewise when the right of the first tenant accrues at a time other than the payment dates of such periodic payments, he shall only receive that portion of such income which amounts to the same percentage thereof as the time during which he has been so entitled is of the total period during which such income would normally accrue; the balance shall be a part of the principal. [Amended in several states.]

Section 5. *(Corporate Dividends and Share Rights.)*

(1) All dividends on shares of a corporation forming a part of the principal which are payable in the shares of the corporation shall be deemed principal. Subject to the provisions of this section, all dividends payable otherwise than in the shares of the corporation itself, including ordinary and extraordinary dividends and dividends payable in shares or other securities or obligations of corporations other than the declaring corporation, shall be deemed income. Where the trustee shall have the option of receiving a dividend either in cash or in the shares of the declaring corporation, it shall be considered as a cash dividend and deemed income, irrespective of the choice made by the trustee.

(2) All rights to subscribe to the shares or other securities or obligations of a corporation accruing on account of the ownership of shares or other securities in such corporation, and the proceeds of any sale of such rights, shall be deemed principal. All rights to subscribe to the shares or other securities or obligations of a corporation accruing on account of the ownership of shares or other securities

in another corporation, and the proceeds of any sale of such rights, shall be deemed income.

(3) Where the assets of a corporation are liquidated, amounts paid upon corporate shares as cash dividends declared before such liquidation occurred or as arrears of preferred or guaranteed dividends shall be deemed income; all other amounts paid upon corporate shares on disbursement of the corporate assets to the stockholders shall be deemed principal. All disbursements of corporate assets to the stockholders, whenever made, which are designated by the corporation as a return of capital or division of corporate property shall be deemed principal.

(4) Where a corporation succeeds another by merger, consolidation or reorganization or otherwise acquires its assets, and the corporate shares of the succeeding corporation are issued to the shareholders of the original corporation in like proportion to, or in substitution for, their shares of the original corporation, the two corporations shall be considered a single corporation in applying the provisions of this section. But two corporations shall not be considered a single corporation under this section merely because one owns corporate shares of or otherwise controls or directs the other.

(5) In applying this section the date when a dividend accrues to the person who is entitled to it shall be held to be the date specified by the corporation as the one on which the stockholders entitled thereto are determined, or in default thereof the date of declaration of the dividend. [Amended in most states.]

Section 6. *(Premium and Discount Bonds.)* Where any part of the principal consists of bonds or other obligations for the payment of money, they shall be deemed principal at their inventory value or in default thereof at their market value at the time the principal was established, or at their cost where purchased later, regardless of their par or maturity value; and upon their respective maturities or upon their sale any loss or gain realized thereon shall fall upon or enure to the principal. [Amended in most states.]

Section 7. *(Principal Used in Business.)*

(1) Whenever a trustee or a tenant is authorized by the terms of the transaction by which the principal was established, or by law, to use any part of the principal in the continuance of a business which the original owner of the property comprising the principal had been carrying on, the net profits of such business attributable to such principal shall be deemed income.

(2) Where such business consists of buying and selling property, the net profits for any period shall be ascertained by deducting from the gross returns during and the inventory value of the property at the end of such period, the expenses during and the inventory value of the property at the beginning of such period.

(3) Where such business does not consist of buying and selling property, the net income shall be computed in accordance with the customary practice of such business, but not in such way as to decrease the principal.

(4) Any increase in the value of the principal used in such business shall be deemed principal, and all losses in any one calendar year, after the income from such business for that year has been exhausted, shall fall upon principal. [Amended in several states.]

Section 8. *(Principal Comprising Animals.)* Where any part of the principal consists of animals employed in business, the provisions of Section 7 shall apply; and in other cases where the animals are held as a part of the principal partly or wholly because of the offspring or increase which they are expected to produce, all offspring or increase shall be deemed principal to the extent necessary to maintain the original number of such animals and the remainder shall be deemed income; and in all other cases such offspring or increase shall be deemed income. [Omitted in several states.]

Section 9. *(Disposition of Natural Resources.)* Where any part of the principal consists of property in lands from which may be taken timber, minerals, oils, gas or other natural resources and the trustee or tenant is authorized by law or by the terms of the transaction by which the principal was established to sell, lease or otherwise develop such natural resources, and no provision is made for the disposition of the net proceeds thereof after the payment of expenses and carrying charges on such property, such proceeds, if received as rent on a lease, shall be deemed income, but if received as consideration, whether as royalties or otherwise, for the permanent severance of such natural resources from the lands, shall be deemed principal to be invested to produce income. Nothing in this section shall be construed to abrogate or extend any right which may otherwise have accrued by law to a tenant to develop or work such natural resources for his own benefit. [Substantially amended in many states.]

Section 10. *(Principal Subject to Depletion.)* Where any part of the principal consists of property subject to depletion, such as leaseholds, patents, copyrights and royalty rights, and the trustee or tenant in possession is not under a duty to change the form of the investment of the principal, the full amount of rents, royalties or return from the property shall be income to the tenant; but where the trustee or tenant is under a duty, arising either by law or by the terms of the transaction by which the principal was established, to change the form of the investment, either at once or as soon as it may be done without loss, then the return from such property not in excess of [five] per centum per annum of its fair inventory value or in default thereof its market value at the time the principal was established, or at its cost where purchased later, shall be deemed income and the remainder principal. [Omitted in several states; amended in several.]

Section 11. *(Unproductive Estate.)*

(1) Where any part of a principal in the possession of a trustee consists of realty or personalty which for more than a year and until disposed of as hereinafter stated has not produced an average net income of at least one per centum per annum of its fair inventory value or in default thereof its market value at the time the principal was established or of its cost where purchased later, and the trustee is under a duty to change the form of the investment as soon as it may be done without sacrifice of value and such change is delayed, but is made before the principal is finally distributed, then the tenant, or in case of his death his personal representative, shall be entitled to share in the net proceeds received from the property as delayed income to the extent hereinafter stated.

(2) Such income shall be the difference between the net proceeds received from the property and the amount which, had it been placed at simple interest at the rate of [five] per centum per annum for the period during which the change was delayed, would have produced the net proceeds at the time of change, but in no event shall such income be more than the amount by which the net proceeds exceed the fair inventory value of the property or in default thereof its market value at the time the principal was established or its cost where purchased later. The net proceeds shall consist of the gross proceeds received from the property less any expenses incurred in disposing of it and less all carrying charges which have been paid out of principal during the period while it has been unproductive.

(3) The change shall be taken to have been delayed from the time when the duty to make it first arose, which shall be presumed, in the absence of evidence to the contrary, to be one year after the trustee first received the property if then unproductive, otherwise one year after it became unproductive.

(4) If the tenant has received any income from the property or has had any beneficial use thereof during the period while the change has been delayed, his share of the delayed income shall be reduced by the amount of such income received or the value of the use had.

(5) In the case of successive tenants the delayed income shall be divided among them or their representatives according to the length of the period for which each was entitled to income. [Omitted in several states; amended in many.]

Section 12. *(Expenses—Trust Estates.)*

(1) All ordinary expenses incurred in connection with the trust estate or with its administration and management, including regularly recurring taxes assessed against any portion of the principal, water rates, premiums on insurance taken upon the estates of both tenant and remainderman, interest on mortgages on the principal, ordinary repairs, trustees' compensation except commissions computed on principal, compensation of assistants, and court costs and attorneys' and other fees on regular accountings, shall be paid out of income. But such expenses

where incurred in disposing of, or as carrying charges on, unproductive estate as defined in Section 11, shall be paid out of principal, subject to the provisions of Subsection (2) of Section 11.

(2) All other expenses, including trustee's commissions computed upon principal, cost of investing or reinvesting principal, attorneys' fees and other costs incurred in maintaining or defending any action to protect the trust or the property or assure the title thereof, unless due to the fault or cause of the tenant, and costs of, or assessments for, improvements to property forming part of the principal, shall be paid out of principal. Any tax levied by any authority, federal, state or foreign, upon profit or gain defined as principal under the terms of Subsection (2) of Section 3 shall be paid out of principal, notwithstanding said tax may be denominated a tax upon income by the taxing authority.

(3) Expenses paid out of income according to Subsection (1) which represent regularly recurring charges shall be considered to have accrued from day to day, and shall be apportioned on that basis whenever the right of the tenant begins or ends at some date other than the payment date of the expenses. Where the expenses to be paid out of income are of unusual amount, the trustee may distribute them throughout an entire year or part thereof, or throughout a series of years. After such distribution, where the right of the tenant ends during the period, the expenses shall be apportioned between tenant and remainderman on the basis of such distribution.

(4) Where the costs of, or special taxes or assessments for, an improvement representing an addition of value to property held by the trustee as part of principal are paid out of principal, as provided in Subsection (2), the trustee shall reserve out of income and add to the principal each year a sum equal to the cost of the improvement divided by the number of years of the reasonably expected duration of the improvement. [Amended in most states.]

Section 13. *(Expenses—Non-Trust Estates.)*

(1) The provisions of Section 12, so far as applicable and excepting those dealing with costs of, or special taxes or assessments for, improvements to property, shall govern the apportionment of expenses between tenants and remaindermen where no trust has been created, subject, however, to any legal agreement of the parties or any specific direction of the taxing or other statutes; but where either tenant or remainderman has incurred an expense for the benefit of his own estate and without the consent or agreement of the other, he shall pay such expense in full.

(2) Subject to the exceptions stated in Subsection (1) the cost of, or special taxes or assessments for, an improvement representing an addition of value to property forming part of the principal shall be paid by the tenant, where such improvement cannot reasonably be expected to outlast the estate of the tenant. In all other cases a portion thereof only shall be paid by the tenant, while the re-

mainder shall be paid by the remainderman. Such portion shall be ascertained by taking that percentage of the total which is found by dividing the present value of the tenant's estate by the present value of an estate of the same form as that of the tenant except that it is limited for a period corresponding to the reasonably expected duration of the improvement. The computation of present values of the estates shall be made on the expectancy basis set forth in the [American Experience Tables of Mortality] and no other evidence of duration or expectancy shall be considered. [Omitted in several states; amended in several.]

Section 14. *(Uniformity of Interpretation.)* This act shall be so interpreted and construed as to effectuate its general purpose to make uniform the law of those states which enact it.

Section 15. *(Short Title.)* This act may be cited as the Uniform Principal and Income Act.

Section 16. *(Repeal.)* [All acts or parts of acts which are inconsistent with the provisions of this act] are hereby repealed.

Section 17. *(Time of Taking Effect.)* This act shall take effect . . and shall apply to all estates of tenants or remaindermen which become legally effective after that date.

APPENDIX Four

Revised Uniform Principal and Income Act*

Sec.

---

*Drafted for the National Conference of Commissioners on Uniform State Laws by Allison Dunham. Approved 1962. Adopted in Arkansas, California, Florida, Hawaii, Idaho, Indiana, Kansas, Maryland, Michigan, Minnesota, Mississippi, Nevada, New Mexico, New York, North Carolina, North Dakota, Oregon, South Carolina, Utah, Washington, Wisconsin, Wyoming.

Section 1. *(Definitions.)* As used in this Act:

(1) "income beneficiary" means the person to whom income is presently payable or for whom it is accumulated for distribution as income;

(2) "inventory value" means the cost of property purchased by the trustee and the market value of other property at the time it became subject to the trust, but in the case of a testamentary trust the trustee may use any value finally determined for the purposes of an estate or inheritance tax;

(3) "remainderman" means the person entitled to principal, including income which has been accumulated and added to principal;

(4) "trustee" means an original trustee and any successor or added trustee. (Amended in two states.)

Section 2. *(Duty of Trustee as to Receipts and Expenditures.)*

(a) A trust shall be administered with due regard to the respective interests of income beneficiaries and remaindermen. A trust is so administered with respect to the allocation of receipts and expenditures if a receipt is credited or an expenditure is charged to income or principal or partly to each—

(1) in accordance with the terms of the trust instrument, notwithstanding contrary provisions of this Act;

(2) in the absence of any contrary terms of the trust instrument, in accordance with the provisions of this Act; or

(3) if neither of the preceding rules of administration is applicable, in accordance with what is reasonable and equitable in view of the interests of those entitled to income as well as of those entitled to principal, and in view of the manner in which men of ordinary prudence, discretion and judgment would act in the management of their own affairs.

(b) If the trust instrument gives the trustee discretion in crediting a receipt or charging an expenditure to income or principal or partly to each, no inference of imprudence or partiality arises from the fact that the trustee has made an allocation contrary to a provision of this Act.

Section 3. *(Income; Principal; Charges.)*

(a) Income is the return in money or property derived from the use of principal, including return received as

(1) rent of real or personal property, including sums received for cancellation or renewal of a lease;

(2) interest on money lent, including sums received as consideration for the privilege of prepayment of principal except as provided in section 7 on bond premium and bond discount;

(3) income earned during administration of a decedent's estate as provided in section 5;

(4) corporate distributions as provided in section 6;

(5) accrued increment on bonds or other obligations issued at discount as provided in section 7;

(6) receipts from business and farming operations as provided in section 8;

(7) receipts from disposition of natural resources as provided in sections 9 and 10;

(8) receipts from other principal subject to depletion as provided in section 11;

(9) receipts from disposition of underproductive property as provided in section 12.

(b) Principal is the property which has been set aside by the owner or the person legally empowered so that it is held in trust eventually to be delivered to a remainderman while the return or use of the principal is in the meantime taken or received by or held for accumulation for an income beneficiary. Principal includes

(1) consideration received by the trustee on the sale or other transfer of principal or on repayment of a loan or as a refund or replacement or change in the form of principal;

(2) proceeds of property taken on eminent domain proceedings;

(3) proceeds of insurance upon property forming part of the principal except proceeds of insurance upon a separate interest of an income beneficiary;

(4) stock dividends, receipts on liquidation of a corporation, and other corporate distributions as provided in section 6;

(5) receipts from the disposition of corporate securities as provided in section 7;

(6) royalties and other receipts from disposition of natural resources as provided in sections 9 and 10;

(7) receipts from other principal subject to depletion as provided in section 11;

(8) any profit resulting from any change in the form of principal except as provided in section 12 on underproductive property;

(9) receipts from disposition of underproductive property as provided in section 12;

(10) any allowances for depreciation established under sections 8 and 13(a) (2).

(c) After determining income and principal in accordance with the terms of the trust instrument or of this Act, the trustee shall charge to income or principal expenses and other charges as provided in section 13. [Amended in two states.]

Section 4. *(When Right to Income Arises; Apportionment of Income.)*

(a) An income beneficiary is entitled to income from the date specified in the trust instrument, or, if none is specified, from the date an asset becomes subject to the trust. In the case of an asset becoming subject to a trust by reason of a will, it becomes subject to the trust as of the date of the death of the testator even though there is an intervening period of administration of the testator's estate.

(b) In the administration of a decedent's estate or an asset becoming subject to a trust by reason of a will

(1) receipts due but not paid at the date of death of the testator are principal;

(2) receipts in the form of periodic payments (other than corporate distributions to stockholders), including rent, interest, or annuities, not due at the date of the death of the testator shall be treated as accruing from day to day. That portion of the receipt accruing before the date of death is principal, and the balance is income.

(c) In all other cases, any receipt from an income producing asset is income even though the receipt was earned or accrued in whole or in part before the date when the asset became subject to the trust.

(d) On termination of an income interest, the income beneficiary whose interest is terminated, or his estate, is entitled to

(1) income undistributed on the date of termination;

(2) income due but not paid to the trustee on the date of termination;

(3) income in the form of periodic payments (other than corporate distributions to stockholders), including rent, interest, or annuities, not due on the date of termination, accrued from day to day.

(e) Corporate distributions to stockholders shall be treated as due on the day fixed by the corporation for determination of stockholders of record entitled to distribution or, if no date is fixed, on the date of declaration of the distribution by the corporation. [Amended in two states.]

Section 5. *(Income Earned During Administration of a Decedent's Estate.)*

(a) Unless the will otherwise provides and subject to subsection (b), all expenses incurred in connection with the settlement of a decedent's estate, including debts, funeral expenses, estate taxes, interest and penalties concerning taxes, family allowances, fees of attorneys and personal representatives, and court costs shall be charged against the principal of the estate.

(b) Unless the will otherwise provides, income from the assets of a decedent's estate after the death of the testator and before distribution, including income from property used to discharge liabilities, shall be determined in accordance with the rules applicable to a trustee under this Act and distributed as follows:

(1) to specific legatees and devisees, the income from the property bequeathed or devised to them respectively, less taxes, ordinary repairs, and other expenses of management and operation of the property, and an appropriate portion of interest accrued since the death of the testator and of taxes imposed on income (excluding taxes on capital gains) which accrue during the period of administration;

(2) to all other legatees and devisees, except legatees of pecuniary bequests not in trust, the balance of the income, less the balance of taxes, ordinary repairs, and other expenses of management and operation of all property from which the estate is entitled to income, interest accrued since the death of the testator, and taxes imposed on income (excluding taxes on capital gains) which accrue during the period of administration, in proportion to their respective interests in the undistributed assets of the estate computed at times of distribution on the basis of inventory value.

(c) Income received by a trustee under subsection (b) shall be treated as income of the trust. [Amended in two states.]

Section 6. *(Corporate Distributors.)*

(a) Corporate distributions of shares of the distributing corporation, including distributions in the form of a stock split or stock dividend, are principal. A right to subscribe to shares or other securities issued by the distributing corporation accruing to stockholders on account of their stock ownership and the proceeds of any sale of the right are principal.

(b) Except to the extent that the corporation indicates that some part of a corporate distribution is a settlement of preferred or guaranteed dividends accrued since the trustee became a stockholder or is in lieu of an ordinary cash dividend, a corporate distribution is principal if the distribution is pursuant to

(1) a call of shares;

(2) a merger, consolidation, reorganization, or other plan by which assets of the corporation are acquired by another corporation; or

(3) a total or partial liquidation of the corporation, including any distribution which the corporation indicates is a distribution in total or partial liquidation or any distribution of assets, other than cash, pursuant to a court decree or final administrative order by a government agency ordering distribution of the particular assets.

(c) Distributions made from ordinary income by a regulated investment company or by a trust qualifying and electing to be taxed under federal law as a real estate investment trust are income. All other distributions made by the company or trust, including distributions from capital gains, depreciation, or depletion, whether or in the form of cash or an option to take new stock or cash or an option to purchase additional shares, are principal.

(d) Except as provided in subsections (a), (b), and (c), all corporate distributions are income, including cash dividends, distributions of or rights to subscribe to shares or securities or obligations of corporations other than the distributing corporation, and the proceeds of the rights or property distributions. Except as provided in subsections (b) and (c), if the distributing corporation gives a stockholder an option to receive a distribution either in cash or in its own shares, the distribution chosen is income.

(e) The trustee may rely upon any statement of the distributing corporation as to any fact relevant under any provision of this Act concerning the source or character of dividends or distributions of corporate assets. [Substantially amended in two states.]

Section 7. *(Bond Premium and Discount.)*

(a) Bonds or other obligations for the payment of money are principal at their inventory value, except as provided in subsection (b) for discount bonds. No provision shall be made for amortization of bond premiums or for accumulation for discount. The proceeds of sale, redemption, or other disposition of the bonds or obligations are principal.

(b) The increment in value of a bond or other obligation for the payment of money payable at a future time in accordance with a fixed schedule of appreciation in excess of the price at which it was issued is distributable as income. The increment in value is distributable to the beneficiary who was the income beneficiary at the time of increment from the first principal cash available or, if none is available, when realized by sale, redemption, or other disposition. Whenever unrealized increment is distributed as income but out of principal, the principal shall be reimbursed for the increment when realized. [Amended in two states.]

Section 8. *(Business and Farming Operations.)*

(a) If a trustee uses any part of the principal in the continuance of a business of which the settlor was a sole proprietor or a partner, the net profits of the business, computed in accordance with generally accepted accounting principles for a comparable business, are income. If a loss results in any fiscal or calendar year, the loss falls on principal and shall not be carried into any other fiscal or calendar year for purposes of calculating net income.

(b) Generally accepted accounting principles shall be used to determine income from an agricultural or farming operation, including the raising of animals or the operation of a nursery.

Section 9. *(Disposition of Natural Resources.)*

(a) If any part of the principal consists of a right to receive royalties, overriding or limited royalties, working interests, production payments, net profit interests, or other interests in minerals or other natural resources in, on or under land, the receipts from taking the natural resources from the land shall be allocated as follows:

(1) If received as rent on a lease or extension payments on a lease, the receipts are income.

(2) If received from a production payment, the receipts are income to the extent of any factor for interest or its equivalent provided in the governing instrument. There shall be allocated to principal the fraction of the balance of the receipts which the unrecovered cost of the production payments bears to the balance owed on the production payment, exclusive of any factor for interest or its equivalent. The receipts not allocated to principal are income.

(3) If received as a royalty, overriding or limited royalty, or bonus, or from a working, net profit, or any other interest in minerals or other natural resources, receipts not provided for in the preceding paragraphs of this section shall be apportioned on a yearly basis in accordance with this paragraph whether or not any natural resource was being taken from the land at the time the trust was established. Twenty-seven and one-half per cent of the gross receipts (but not to exceed 50% of the net receipts remaining after payment of all expenses, direct and indirect, computed without allowance for depletion) shall be added to principal as an allowance for depletion. The balance of the gross receipts, after payment therefrom of all expenses, direct and indirect, is income.

(b) If a trustee, on the effective date of this Act, held an item of depletable property of a type specified in this section he shall allocate receipts from the property in the manner used before the effective date of this Act, but as to all depletable property acquired after the effective date of this Act by an existing or new trust, the method of allocation provided herein shall be used.

(c) This section does not apply to timber, water, soil, sod, dirt, turf, or mosses.

Section 10. *(Timber.)* If any part of the principal consists of land from which merchantable timber may be removed, the receipts from taking the timber from the land shall be allocated in accordance with section 2(a) (3). [Omitted in one state.]

Section 11. *(Other Property Subject to Depletion.)* Except as provided in sections 9 and 10, if the principal consists of property subject to depletion, including leaseholds, patents, copyrights, royalty rights, and rights to receive payments on a contract for deferred compensation, receipts from the property, not in excess of 5% per year of its inventory value, are income, and the balancc is principal. [Substantially amended in two states.]

Section 12. *(Underproductive Property.)*

(a) Except as otherwise provided in this section, a portion of the net proceeds of sale of any part of principal which has not produced an average net income of at least 1% per year of its inventory value for more than a year (including as income the value of any beneficial use of the property by the income beneficiary) shall be treated as delayed income to which the income beneficiary is entitled as provided in this section. The net proceeds of sale are the gross proceeds received, including the value of any property received in substitution for the property disposed of, less the expenses, including capital gains tax, if any, incurred in disposition and less any carrying charge paid while the property was underprotective.

(b) The sum allocated as delayed income is the difference between the net proceeds and the amount which, had it been invested at simple interest at [4%] per year while the property was underproductive, would have produced the net proceeds. This sum, plus any carrying charges and expenses previously charged against income while the property was underproductive, less any income received by the income beneficiary from the property and less the value of any beneficial use of the property by the income beneficiary, is income, and the balance is principal.

(c) An income beneficiary or his estate is entitled to delayed income under this section as if it accrued from day to day during the time he was a beneficiary.

(d) If principal subject to this section is disposed of by conversion into property which cannot be apportioned easily, including land or mortgages (for example, realty acquired by or in lieu of foreclosure), the income beneficiary is entitled to the net income from any property or obligation into which the original principal is converted while the substituted property or obligation is held. If within 5 years after the conversion the substituted property has not been further converted into easily apportionable property, no allocation as provided in this section shall be made. [Omitted in one state; substantially amended in one.]

Section 13. *(Charges Against Income and Principal.)*

(a) The following charges shall be made against income:

(1) ordinary expenses incurred in connection with the administration, management, or preservation of the trust property, including regularly recurring taxes assessed against any portion of the principal, water rates, premiums on insurance taken upon the interests of the income beneficiary, remainderman, or trustee, interest paid by the trustee, and ordinary repairs;

(2) a reasonable allowance for depreciation on property subject to depreciation under generally accepted accounting principles, but no allowance shall be made for depreciation of that portion of any real property used by a beneficiary as a residence or for depreciation of any property held by the trustee on the effective date of this Act for which the trustee is not then making an allowance for depreciation;

(3) one-half of court costs, attorney's fees, and other fees on periodic judicial accounting, unless the court directs otherwise;

(4) court costs, attorney's fees, and other fees on other accountings or judicial proceedings if the matter primarily concerns the income interest, unless the court directs otherwise;

(5) one-half of the trustee's regular compensation, whether based on a percentage of principal or income, and all expenses reasonably incurred for current management of principal and application of income;

(6) any tax levied upon receipts defined as income under this Act or the trust instrument and payable by the trustee.

(b) If charges against income are of unusual amount, the trustee may by means of reserves or other reasonable means charge them over a reasonable period of time and withhold from distribution sufficient sums to regularize distributions.

(c) The following charges shall be made against principal:

(1) trustee's compensation not chargeable to income under subsections (a) (4) and (a) (5), special compensation of trustees, expenses reasonably incurred in connection with principal, court costs and attorney's fees primarily

concerning matters of principal, and trustee's compensation computed on principal as an acceptance, distribution, or termination fee;

(2) charges not provided for in subsection (a), including the cost of investing and reinvesting principal, the payments on principal of an indebtedness (including a mortgage amortized by periodic payments of principal), expenses for preparation of property for rental or sale, and, unless the court directs otherwise, expenses incurred in maintaining or defending any action to construe the trust or protect it or the property or assure the title of any trust property;

(3) extraordinary repairs or expenses incurred in making a capital improvement to principal, including special assessments, but, a trustee may establish an allowance for depreciation out of income to the extent permitted by subsection (a) (2) and by section 8;

(4) any tax levied upon profit, gain, or other receipts allocated to principal notwithstanding denomination of the tax as an income tax by the taxing authority;

(5) if an estate or inheritance tax is levied in respect of a trust in which both an income beneficiary and a remainderman have an interest, any amount apportioned to the trust, including interest and penalties, even though the income beneficiary also has rights in the principal.

(d) Regularly recurring charges payable from income shall be apportioned to the same extent and in the same manner that income is apportioned under section 4. [Substantially amended in two states.]

Section 14. *(Application of Act.)* Except as specifically provided in the trust instrument or the will or in this Act, this Act shall apply to any receipt or expense received or incurred after the effective date of this Act by any trust or decedent's estate whether established before or after the effective date of this Act and whether the asset involved was acquired by the trustee before or after the effective date of this Act.

Section 15. *(Uniformity of Interpretation.)* This Act shall be so construed as to effectuate its general purpose to make uniform the law of those states which enact it.

Section 16. *(Short Title.)* This Act may be cited as the Revised Uniform Principal and Income Act.

Section 17. *(Severability.)* If any provision of this Act or the application thereof to any person or circumstance is held invalid, the invalidity does not affect other provisions or applications of the Act which can be given effect without the invalid provision or application and to this end the provisions of this Act are severable.

Section 18. *(Repeal.)* [The following acts and parts of acts are repealed: [   ].

Section 19. *(Time of Taking Effect.)* This Act shall take effect on ____.

APPENDIX **Five**

Uniform Trustees' Accounting Act*

Sec.

---

* This Act has been withdrawn but is included here as a reference for the general information and definitions it contains.

Section 1. *(Definition of Terms.)* As used in this Act: A "testamentary trustee" means a trustee serving under a trust created by a will of a testator domiciled in this state at the time of his death whose will has been admitted to probate in this state, whether the trustee was appointed by the testator or by a court or other authority.

A "non-testamentary trustee" means a trustee serving under a trust created in this state otherwise than by a will, whether the trustee was appointed by the settlor or by a court or other authority.

The word "trustee" includes trustees, a corporate as well as a natural person, a successor or substitute trustee, and the successor in interest of a deceased sole trustee.

"Beneficiary" includes a beneficiary under the trust, a person who is entitled to the trust capital at the termination of the trust and a surety on the bond of the trustee.

"Settlor" includes the creator of a testamentary as well as a non-testamentary trust.

"Relative" means a spouse, ancestor, descendant, brother, or sister.

"Affiliate" means any person directly or indirectly controlling or controlled by another person, or any person under direct or indirect common control with another person. It includes any person with whom a trustee has an express or implied agreement regarding the purchase of trust investments by each from the other, directly or indirectly.

This Act shall not apply to resulting trusts, constructive trusts, business trusts where certificates of beneficial interest are issued to the beneficiaries, investment trusts, voting trusts, insurance trusts prior to the death of the insured, trusts in the nature of mortgages or pledges, trusts created by judgment or decree of a federal court or a state court other than the [probate court], liquidation trusts, or trust for the sole purpose of paying dividends, interest or interest coupons, salaries, wages or pensions. [Omitted in one state; amended in one.]

(Testamentary Trusts, Sections 2–11, inclusive)

Section 2. *(Testamentary Trust Inventory.)* Within thirty days after it is the duty of the first qualifying testamentary trustee to take possession of the trust property he shall file with the [probate court where the will was admitted to probate] an inventory under oath, showing by items all the trust property which shall have come to his possession or knowledge.

Section 3. *(Intermediate Accountings.)* Within thirty days after the expiration of the first year after the first qualifying testamentary trustee was under a duty to file his inventory as prescribed in Section 2 the testamentary trustee then in office shall file with the [probate court of the county where the will was admitted to probate] an intermediate account under oath covering such year and showing:

(a) the period which the account covers;

(b) the names and addresses of the living beneficiaries known to the trustee, with a statement as to those known to be minors or under legally declared disability; and a description of any possible unborn or unascertained beneficiaries; and the name of the surety or sureties on the trustee's bond with the amount of such bond;

(c) in a separate schedule the trust principal on hand at the beginning of the accounting period and the then status of its investment; the investments received from the settlor and still held; additions to trust principal during the accounting period with the dates and sources of acquisitions; investments collected, sold or charged off during the accounting period, with the consequent loss or gain and whether credited to principal or income; investments made during the accounting period, with the date, source and cost of each; deductions from principal during the accounting period, with the date and purpose of each; and trust principal on hand at the end of the accounting period, how invested, and the estimated market value of each investment;

(d) in a separate schedule the trust income on hand at the beginning of the accounting period, and in what form held; trust income received during the accounting period, when, and from what source; trust income paid out during the accounting period, when, to whom, and for what purpose; trust income on hand at the end of the accounting period, and how invested;

(e) that neither any seller of, nor buyer from, the trustee of trust property during the accounting period was at the time of such sale or purchase (1) in the case of a corporate trustee an affiliate, or an officer, employee, or nominee of the trustee or of an affiliate; or was (2) in the case of a noncorporate trustee a relative, partner, employer, employee, or business associate; but none of the provisions of this subsection shall apply to purchases and sales made by brokers for the trustee or to stock exchanges;

(f) a statement of unpaid claims with the reason for failure to pay them, including a statement as to whether any estate or inheritance taxes have become due with regard to the trust property, and if due, whether paid;

(g) a brief summary of the account;

(h) such other facts as the court may by rule or court order require.

Within thirty days after the end of each yearly period thereafter during the life of the trust the testamentary trustee then in office shall file with the same court an intermediate account under oath showing corresponding facts regarding the current accounting period. [Amended in two states.]

Section 4. *(Final Accounting.)* Within [   ] days after the termination of every testamentary trust the trustee, and in the case of the transfer of the trusteeship due to the death, resignation, removal, dissolution, merger or consolidation of a sole trustee the successor in interest of the old trustee, shall file with the [probate court of the county where the will was admitted to probate] a final account under oath, showing for the period since the filing of the last account the facts required by Section 3 regarding intermediate accountings and in case of termination of the trust the distribution of the trust property which the accountant proposes to make. [Amended in all states.]

Section 5. *(Distribution Accounting.)* Within [   ] days after the distribution of the trust property by the testamentary trustee he shall file in the court where the final account was filed a distribution account of the trust property which he has distributed and the receipts of the distributees. [Amended in all states.]

Section 6. *(Procedure on Intermediate Accountings.)* Every testamentary trustee who files an intermediate account in court shall within ten days after such filing deliver to each known beneficiary a notice of such filing, and if there is to be no court hearing on the account a summary of the account with an offer to deliver the full account on demand, or if there is to be a court hearing on the account a copy of the account. Such delivery may be (1) by handing the notice or copy to the beneficiary personally, or to his guardian, or attorney of record; or (2) by sending it by registered mail with return receipt requested to such beneficiary, or his guardian or attorney of record, at the last known address of the addressee. Any beneficiary or the trustee may petition the court for a hearing on any intermediate account, and the holding of such a hearing shall be in the discretion of the court. In the case of the third intermediate accounting and every three years thereafter the trustee shall apply to the court for a hearing on and approval of all unapproved accounts and shall give each known beneficiary written notice of such application [   ] days before the return day thereof, in the manner prescribed for the delivery of the copy of the account. The return day of the application for a hearing on an intermediate accounting shall be at least [   ] days after the latest account was filed. The notice by the trustee of the application for a hearing on and approval of the account shall inform the beneficiaries of the amount of commissions or other compensation to be requested by the trustee on such hearing, and the amount of other fees which the court will then be requested to allow. [Omitted in one state; amended in all others.]

Section 7. *(Service of Papers in Final Accounting.)* At least [   ] days before the return day of a final accounting the testamentary trustee shall deliver to each beneficiary a copy of the account and a notice of the time and place at which the account will be presented for approval, which date shall not be earlier than [   ] days after the account was filed. Such delivery may be accomplished in the same manner as with regard to the service of papers on the intermediate accounting. The notice shall inform the beneficiaries of the amount of commissions or other compensation to be requested by the trustee on the application for approval of the account, and the amount of other fees which the court will then be requested to allow. [Omitted in one state; amended in all others.]

Section 8. *(Vouchers.)* When an intermediate or final account is presented for consideration in court the testamentary trustee shall produce in court vouchers for all expenditures of $20 or more, made by the trustee during the accounting period. [The vouchers shall be returned to the trustee after the account is approved.] [Omitted in one state; amended in all others.]

Section 9. *(Representation.)* Any beneficiary who is an infant, of unsound mind or otherwise legally incompetent, and also possible unborn or unascertained beneficiaries may be represented in a testamentary trust accounting by the court, or by competent living members of the class to which they do or would belong, or by a guardian *ad litem,* as the court deems best. If the residence of any beneficiary is unknown, or there is doubt as to the existence of one or more persons as beneficiaries, the court shall make such provision for service of notice and representation on the accounting as it believes proper. [Amended in one state.]

Section 10. *(Court Action.)* On the return day of an application for a hearing on and approval of an intermediate or final account the testamentary trustee shall file an affidavit proving the timely delivery to the known beneficiaries of the documents required by the Act or by court order. The procedure as to filing of objections, examination of the trustee and other witnesses, inspection of the trust property, adjournments, reference to a master or other representative of the court, amendment of the account, and similar matters, shall be in the discretion of the court. The court shall, as soon as practicable, act upon the account, and discharge the trustee if the account is an approved distribution account. [Amended in one state.]

Section 11. *(Effect of Court Approval.)* The approval by the court of a testamentary trustee's account after due notice and service of papers or representation as provided in this Act, shall, subject to the right of appeal, relieve the trustee and his sureties from liability to all beneficiaries then known or in being, or who thereafter become known or in being, for all the trustee's acts and omissions which are fully and accurately described in the account, including the then investment of the trust funds. The court may disapprove the account and surcharge the trustee for any loss caused by a breach of trust committed by him. The account may be reopened by the court on motion of the trustee or a beneficiary, for amendment or revision, if it later appears that the account is incorrect, either because of fraud or mistake. Court approvals or disapprovals of intermediate or final accounts shall be deemed final judgements in so far as the right of appeal is concerned. [No account shall be reopened because of a mistake more than one year after its approval. No beneficiary may move for the reopening of any account because of fraud more than [   ] days after he discovers the existence of the fraud.] [Amended in all states.]

(Non-Testamentary Trusts, Sections 12 and 13.)

Section 12. *(Inventory by Non-Testamentary Trustee.)* Within thirty days after it is the duty of the first qualifying trustee of a non-testamentary trust to take possession of the trust property he shall file in the office of the [Clerk of the   ] court in the county where the trust was created a notice of his appointment as trustee, a copy of the instrument creating the trust if the trust was created by a writing, a list of the names, addresses, and dates of birth of the known living beneficiaries, a description of any possible unborn or unascertained beneficiaries, and an inventory under oath of the trust property which shall have come to his possession or knowledge. [Amended in two states.]

Section 13. *(Accounting by Non-Testamentary Trustee.)* Every non-testamentary trustee shall file intermediate, final and distribution accounts with the [Clerk of the   ] court in the county where the trust was created, at the same intervals, under the same conditions, and with the same effect as herein provided with respect to the accountings of a testamentary trustee in the [probate] court. [Amended in two states.]

(General Provisions, Sections 14 to 27, inclusive.)

Section 14. *(Duties of Court and Clerks.)* The clerks of the [probate and equity courts] shall severally keep records of all trust inventories and accounts filed with their respective courts and shall within thirty (30) days after the filing should have occurred notify the respective judges of their courts of all failures by trustees to file accounts in accordance with this Act. Such courts shall, upon learning that a trustee subject to their respective jurisdictions has failed to perform any duty placed upon him by this Act, issue a citation or order to the trustee requiring him to perform such duty. [Omitted or amended in two states.]

Section 15. *(Power of Settlor.)* The settlor of any trust affected by this Act may, by provision in the instrument creating the trust if the trust was created by a writing, or by oral statement to the trustee at the time of the creation of the trust if the trust was created orally, or by an amendment of the trust if the settlor reserved the power to amend the trust, relieve his trustee from any or all of the duties which would otherwise be placed upon him by this Act, or add duties to those imposed by this Act on his trustee with regard to inventories and accountings. But no expression of intent by any settlor shall affect the jurisdiction of the courts of this State over inventories and accounts of trustees, in so far as such jurisdiction does not depend upon the provisions of this Act. [Amended in one state.]

Section 16. *(Power of Beneficiary.)* Any beneficiary, if of full age and sound mind, may, if acting upon full information, by written instrument delivered to the trustee, excuse the trustee as to such beneficiary from performing any of the duties imposed on him by this Act or exempt the trustee from liability to such beneficiary for failure to perform any of the duties imposed upon the trustee by the terms of this Act. [Amended in one state.]

Section 17. *(Accountability at Other Times.)* Nothing herein contained shall be construed to abridge the power of any court of competent jurisdiction to require testamentary or non-testamentary trustees to file an inventory, to account, to exhibit the trust property, or to give beneficiaries information or the privilege of inspection of trust records and papers, at times other than those herein prescribed; and nothing herein contained shall be construed to abridge the power of such court for cause shown to excuse a trustee from performing any or all of the duties imposed on him by this Act. Nothing herein contained shall prevent the trustee from accounting voluntarily when it is reasonably necessary, even though he is not required to do so by this Act or by court order.

Section 18. *(Enforcement.)* Any beneficiary may apply to a court of competent jurisdiction for an order requiring the trustee to perform the duties imposed upon him by this Act.

Section 19. *(Penalties for Violation of Act.)* When a trustee fails to perform any of the duties imposed upon him by this Act he may be removed, his compensation may be reduced or forfeited, or other civil penalty inflicted, in the discretion of the court.

Section 20. *(Forms of Inventories and Accounts.)* The courts given jurisdiction over accountings by this Act may prescribe forms in which inventories and accounts shall be presented. [Omitted in one state.]

Section 21. *(Oaths.)* Whenever an oath or affirmation is required of a trustee under this Act it may be made in the case of a corporate trustee by an officer of such corporate trustee, and in the case of co-trustees acting jointly by any one of the co-trustees. [Amended in one state.]

Section 22. *(Charitable Trusts.)* This Act shall apply to charitable trusts. Documents required to be delivered to beneficiaries of such trusts shall be delivered to the [Attorney General of the State and the State Department of Charities]. [Amended in two states.]

Section 23. *(Uniformity of Interpretation.)* This Act shall be so interpreted and construed as to effectuate its general purpose to make uniform the law of those states which enact it.

Section 24. *(Short Title.)* This Act shall be cited as the Uniform Trustees' Accounting Act.

Section 25. *(Severability.)* If any provision of this Act or the application thereof to any person or circumstances is held invalid, such invalidity shall not affect other provisions or applications of the Act which can be given effect without the invalid provision or application, and to this end the provisions of this Act are declared to be severable.

Section 26. *(Repeal.)* All acts or parts of acts which are inconsistent with the provisions of this Act are hereby repealed.

Section 27. *(Time of Taking Effect.)* This Act shall take effect [   ] and shall apply only to testamentary trusts created by wills executed after the effective date of the Act and to non-testamentary trusts created after the effective date of the Act.

APPENDIX **Six**

Statement of Principles
of Trust Institutions*

FOREWARD

This Statement of Principles has been formulated in order that the fundamental principles of institutions engaged in trust business may be restated and thereby become better understood and recognized by the public, as well as by trust institutions, themselves, and in order that it may serve as a guide for trust institutions.

In the conduct of their business trust institutions are governed by the cardinal principle that is common to all fiduciary relationships—namely, fidelity. Policies predicated upon this principle have for their objectives its expression in terms of safety, good management, and personal service. Practices developed under these policies are designed to promote efficiency in administration and operation.

The fact that the services performed by trust institutions have become an integral part of the social and economic structure of the United States makes the principles of such institutions a matter of public interest.

---

*This statement was adopted by the Executive Committee of the Trust Division, American Bankers Association on April 10, 1933, and approved by the Executive Council of the American Bankers Association on April 11, 1933.

ARTICLE I
DEFINITION OF TERMS

Section 1. Trust Institutions.—Trust institutions are corporations engaged in trust business under authority of law. They embrace not only trust companies that are engaged in trust business exclusively but also trust departments of other corporations.

Section 2. Trust Business.—Trust business is the business of settling estates, administering trusts and performing agencies in all appropriate cases for individuals; partnerships; associations; business corporations; public, educational, social, recreational, and charitable institutions; and units of government. It is advisable that a trust institution should limit the functions of its trust department to such services.

ARTICLE II
ACCEPTANCE OF TRUST BUSINESS

A trust institution is under no obligation, either moral or legal, to accept all business that is offered.

Section 1. Personal Trust Business.—With respect to the acceptance of personal trust business the two determining factors are these: Is trust service needed, and can the service be rendered properly? In personal trusts and agencies, the relationship is private, and the trust institution is responsible to those only who have or may have a financial interest in the account.

Section 2. Corporate Trust Business.—In considering the acceptance of a corporate trust or agency the trust institution should be satisfied that the company concerned is in good standing and that the enterprise is of a proper nature.

ARTICLE III
ADMINISTRATION OF TRUST BUSINESS

Section 1. Personal Trusts.—In the administration of its personal trust business, a trust institution should strive at all times to render unexceptionable business and financial service, but it should also be careful to render equally good personal service to beneficiaries. The first duty of a trust institution is to carry out the wishes of the creator of a trust as expressed in the trust instrument. Sympathetic, tactful, personal relationships with immediate beneficiaries are essential to the performance of this duty, keeping in mind also the interest of ultimate beneficiaries. It should be the policy of trust institutions that all personal trusts should be under the direct supervision of and that beneficiaries should be brought into direct contact with the administrative or senior officers of the trust department.

Section 2. Confidential Relationships.—Personal trust service is of a confidential nature and the confidences reposed in a trust department by a customer should never be revealed except when required by law.

Section 3. Fundamental Duties of Trustees.—It is the duty of a trustee to administer a trust solely in the interest of the beneficiaries without permitting the intrusion of interests of the trustee or third parties that may in any way conflict with the interests of the trust; to keep and render accurate accounts with respect to the administration of the trust; to acquaint the beneficiaries with all material facts in connection with the trust; and, in administering the trust, to exercise the care a prudent man familiar with such matters would exercise as trustee of the property of others, adhering to the rule that the trustee is primarily a conserver.

Section 4. Corporate Trust Business.—In the administration of corporate trusts and agencies the trust institution should render the same fine quality of service as it renders in the administration of personal trusts and agencies. Promptness, accuracy, and protection are fundamental requirements of efficient corporate trust service. The terms of the trust instrument should be carried out with scrupulous care and with particular attention to the duties imposed therein upon the trustee for the protection of the security-holders.

ARTICLE IV

OPERATION OF TRUST DEPARTMENTS

Section 1. Separation of Trust Properties.—The properties of each trust should be kept separate from those of all other trusts and separate also from the properties of the trust institution itself.

Section 2. Investment of Trust Funds.—The investment function of a trustee is care and management of property, not mere safekeeping at one extreme or speculation at the other. A trust institution should devote to its trust investments all the care and skill that it has or can reasonably acquire. The responsibility for the investment of trust funds should not be reposed in an individual officer or employee of a trust department. All investments should be made, retained or sold only upon the authority of an investment committee composed of capable and experienced officers or directors of the institution.

When the trust instrument definitely states the investment powers of the trustee, the terms of the instrument must be followed faithfully. If it should become unlawful or impossible or against public policy to follow literally the terms of the trust instrument, the trustee should promptly seek the guidance of the court about varying or interpreting the terms of the instrument and should not act on its own responsibility in this respect except in the face of an emergency, when the guidance of the court beforehand could not be obtained. If the trust instrument is silent about trust investments or if it expressly leaves the selection and retention of trust investments to the judgment and discretion of the trustee, the latter should be governed by considerations of the safety of principal and dependability of income and not by hope or expectation of unusual gain through speculation. However, a trustee should not be content with safety of principal alone to the disregard of the reasonable income requirements of the beneficiaries.

It is a fundamental principle that a trustee should not have any personal financial interest, direct or indirect, in the trust investments, bought for or sold to the trusts of which it is trustee, and that it should not purchase for itself any securities or other property from any of its trusts. Accordingly, it follows that a trust institution should not buy for or sell to its estates or trusts any securities or other property in which it, or its affiliate, has any personal financial interest, and should not purchase for itself, or its affiliate, any securities or other property from its estates or trusts.

ARTICLE V

COMPENSATION FOR TRUST SERVICE

Section 1.—A trust institution is entitled to reasonable compensation for its services. Compensation should be determined on the basis of the cost of the service rendered and the responsibilities assumed. Minimum fees in any community for trust services should be uniform and applied uniformly and impartially to all customers alike.

ARTICLE VI

PROMOTIONAL EFFORT

Section 1. Advertising.—A trust institution has the same right as any other business enterprise to advertise its trust services in appropriate ways. Its advertisements should be dignified and not overstate or overemphasize the qualifications of the trust institutions. There should be no implication that legal services will be rendered. There should be no reflection, expressed or implied, upon other trust institutions or individuals, and the advertisements of all trust institutions should be mutually helpful.

Section 2. Personal Representation.—The propriety of having personal representatives of trust departments is based upon the same principle as that of advertising. Trust business is so individual and distinctive that the customer cannot always obtain from printed matter all he wishes to know about the protection and management the trust institution will give his estate and the services it will render his beneficiaries.

Section 3. New Trust Department.—A corporation should not enter the trust field except with a full appreciation of the responsibilities involved. A new trust department should be established only if there is enough potential trust business within the trade area of the institution to justify the proper personnel and equipment.

Section 4. Entering Corporate Trust Field.—Since the need for trust and agency services to corporations, outside of the centers of population, is much more limited than is that of trust and agency services to individuals, a trust institution should hesitate to enter the corporate trust or agency field unless an actual demand for such services is evident, and the institution is specially equipped to render such service.

ARTICLE VII
RELATIONSHIPS

Section 1. With Public.—Although a trust department is a distinctly private institution in its relations with its customers, it is affected with a public interest in its relations with the community. In its relations with the public a trust institution should be ready and willing to give full information about its own financial responsibility, its staff and equipment, and the safeguards thrown around trust business.

Section 2. With Bar.—Attorneys-at-law constitute a professional group that perform essential functions in relation to trust business, and have a community of interest with trust institutions in the common end of service to the public. The maintenance of harmonious relations between trust institutions and members of the bar is in the best interests of both, and of the public as well. It is a fundamental principle of this relationship that trust institutions should not engage in the practice of law.

Section 3. With Life Underwriters.—Life underwriters also constitute a group having a community of interest with trust institutions in the common purpose of public service. Cooperation between trust institutions and life underwriters is productive of the best mutual service to the public. It is a principle of this cooperation that trust institutions should not engage in the business of selling life insurance.

Index